About the Author

Brian Mayne is a pioneer of personal development for 25 years presenting on a global stage. A founding trainer with the 'Coaching Academy', he is the author of 4 books in 9 languages, UK Speaker of the Year and National Training Award recipient. Brian is also creator of Goal Mapping, with over 1300 certified coaches across 30 countries, reaching more than 4 million people.

Born into a travelling family, Brian left school at 13 without qualifications or the ability to read or write well. Being a natural entrepreneur, he opened a disco when just 19 and became hugely successful, but at age 29 his life crashed leaving him a million pounds in debt, divorced, homeless and unemployed. This tragedy triggered Brian's personal development journey to transform himself and follow his purpose of helping lift 7 million lives with his Mapping System for Success.

His teachings are simple yet profound and employed by schools, coaches and global businesses: Microsoft, Siemens, Disney, Coco-Cola, Barclay's Bank and British Telecom. Anthony Robbins, a world-leading success coach, says:

"Brian is one of the best at helping people create a world-class blueprint for their life – not just goals but sustainable success. His Mapping Systems are a blast and really effective."

This book is the result of my personal journey of Self-discovery and dedicated to everyone who is engaged in their own journey to find their True Self. May this work serve you and point the way to ever-greater happiness, peace and abundance.

SELF MAPPING

A Practical Guide to Discovering Your True Potential

BRIAN MAYNE

WATKINS

Sharing Wisdom Since 1893

This edition first published in the UK and USA 2016 by Watkins,
an imprint of Watkins Media Limited
Unit 11, Shepperton House
89-93 Shepperton Road
London
N1 3DF

3 5 7 9 10 8 6 4

Designed and typeset by Jerry Goldie

Printed and bound in Great Britain

British Library Cataloguing-in-Publication data available

ISBN: 978-1-786782-54-0

www.watkinspublishing.com

www.liftinternational.com

Contents

Who looks outside, dreams.

Who looks inside, awakens.

CARL JUNG

Preface

Everyone has a story to share, a slice of life to speak of. Mine started in 1961 when I was born into a travelling funfair family. After a nomadic childhood in which I had several different homes, schools and sets of friends each year, we finally put down roots on the Isle of Wight where I eventually went on to run our family business. When I was about 30 the business crashed and I lost what seemed like everything: my marriage, my home, my business and many possessions. I wound up massively in debt and, having left school at 13 without any qualifications and challenged with dyslexia, was still relatively unable to read or write.

Life looked pretty bleak and I felt broken, mentally, emotionally, physically. Although I couldn't see it at the time, this was actually the beginning of a new bright, wonderful chapter in my life. Through a chain of synchronicities, I discovered the secret of personal development – the realization that:

You can change the condition of your life by altering the attitude of your heart and mind.

I was shown some very simple but powerful self-improvement techniques and, through their use, felt sheer delight at learning to read and write well just one year later. In many ways I was released from a mental cage and found a new level of freedom. At first I wanted to read everything, just because I could. However, to honour this new gift, I decided to focus on what was helping me most: the study of self-improvement. Everything I learnt that felt right and made sense, I diligently applied to all the various aspects of my self and areas of my life.

A new path began to open up before me, and with each step I took along it, with each insight I gained and aspect of my self I developed, little by little, my circumstances improved.

Little did I know in those early days that I was embarking on a life journey, deeper than I could have imagined, more marvellous than I could have hoped and more joyous than I would have dared to believe. It has been a journey of unfolding truths, of awakening to my true Self, remembering my true purpose and choosing to live from the great fundamental truths of life.

This book represents my earnest endeavour to share the deepest insights, profoundest truths and most helpful lessons that have surfaced on my journey so far. May they serve you greatly, as they have me and the countless thousands of others who have discovered them.

Self-evolution

Be Still, and Know You Are God

Whichever belief system or viewpoint you choose to observe life from, whether physical or spiritual, we could agree that we each come from a place of boundless bliss, total joy and perfect peace. You may choose to believe that is just for nine months of pregnancy, or perhaps for an eternity of spirituality, but for a time we all dwell in a completely nurturing environment where we receive an abundant stream of nourishment, wrapped in wonderful warmth and a feeling of constant connection.

At birth we emerge from this blissful place of *complete comfort* to enter a physical world of extremes: of hot and cold, thirst and hunger, light and dark, pain and pleasure. As we grow we begin to experience limitations and restrictions of movement, expression, communication and choice in a world of relative separation, frustration and isolation. And all the while, even with the most loving of parents and in the most nurturing of environments, we crave that place of complete comfort we knew before, whether you choose to call it the womb, nirvana, spirit, heaven or God.

The Quest for Comfort

At first, our need to satisfy this deep craving will cause us to associate the feeling of comfort with nourishment, stimulation and attention. At the time of writing my baby daughter Ayesha is three months old and has already associated feelings of comfort with cuddles, milk and her dummy. She laughs when she's in comfort and cries when she's not.

As we grow our need for comfort drives us to seek it in admiration, possession and power. In a challenged life where the love is lacking, people often search for comfort in excessive amounts of food, drink, sex or drugs. And while all of these things may bring moments of pleasure, joy and even at times bliss, they never truly satisfy that deep inner yearning at our core and only result in some form of dependency. We are ever chasing the 'comfort dragon'.

In adult life comfort can have many names and take many forms. We don't all take pleasure in the same things and one person's comfort may be another person's pain. When we're in comfort, we take it for granted, as we do the air we breathe. But when we become uncomfortable, in any area of our life, we grab at our objects of comfort as if our life depended on them. Try going without your regular little comforts for a while or, worse still, have them taken away, and see how it makes you want to cry like a baby.

Virtually everyone will chase the comfort dragon in some way: perhaps via comfort food, taking a comfortable job, making a comfortable home, slipping into our comfortable clothes and slippers. We don't stray too far from our comfort zone; we make a comfortable living, so that one day we can be 'very comfortable' in our retirement. The quest for comfort never truly ends.

Sadly, the comfort we find in relationships, possessions, status or power can lead to a kind of addiction, and just as with the drug addict, no amount is ever really enough. The race to keep up never truly ends; most people will spend their entire lives trudging the treadmill of some form of false comfort.

Occasionally, in a fortunate life, we may raise our awareness and find that these pursuits are ultimately unfulfilling. We may undertake more meaningful endeavours such as caring for others, supporting a cause or following a faith. Unfortunately, we tend to carry with us the same flawed mindset and deep cravings for comfort that drove our search in the first place. And, inevitably, we discover that even these worthy aims and ideals don't truly satisfy our deepest and most primal need for comfort at our core.

In truth, it is only by being still and connecting with our essence, the god within, and knowing it as the place from whence we came, that we ever truly find the authentic complete comfort and perfect peace that we crave.

Seeing the True You

To paraphrase the Gospel of Thomas, it is said that 'a man wise in years will not hesitate to look into the eyes of a newborn, and he will marvel'. What does the wise old man marvel at when gazing into the eyes of a baby? He marvels at the pure pristine consciousness, the true Self, the source of complete comfort, as yet unmasked by the ego, from which all life springs and the essence of who a person really is.

> He who amongst you becomes as a child shall know the Kingdom.
> **THE GOSPEL OF THOMAS**

As a parent I can testify that it is not just wise old men, women or adoring parents who are mesmerized by this clear window on the soul. Complete strangers seem drawn to prams in order to gaze into a baby's eyes in wonder.

However, as we grow and begin to experience the world around us, we quickly form mental images of our self and life that start to blur the window. At first our thought-pictures are only fleeting but with time and repetition they solidify into our fixed beliefs and viewpoints. Collectively they create an image of our self that, like an interface or *mask*, forms between our true Self and the world.

Our pictures of understanding work as a personal autopilot, our subconscious self-guidance system that contains a whole movie of images from our past. Together they govern all of our regular repetitive behaviours, enabling us to walk, talk and navigate through the mundane tasks of life without the need for constant conscious attention.

It is our inner mirror – the blueprint of who we think we are – that our subconscious constantly reads in order to keep us the same each and every day. It is amazing, marvellous and almost magical in its operation.

However, this inner image of who you think you are, and its outer physical reflection, your personality, is not your true Self. It is a veil that obscures direct sight of the true you. Life can be limiting or liberating, joyful or despairing, comfortable or uncomfortable depending on the internal picture you have accepted of your self, the mask you wear and how it guides you to think, feel and act in the various areas of your life.

In the 11th century the Sufi mystic Jelaluddin Rumi observed:

> Awhile, as wont may be, self I did claim;
> true Self I did not see, but heard its name.
> I, being self confined, Self did not merit,
> till leaving self behind did Self inherit.

Highs and Lows

We each have two selves: a high Self, which I indicate in these pages with a capital S, and a low self (or ego), indicated with a lower-case s. Notice that Rumi's verses above also make this distinction.

Our high Self descends from Spirit to guide us by way of inspiration and empathy. It is infinite, the seat of our soul and source of our divinity. Representing all of our finest humanitarian qualities, our high Self is our connection to the All. It is the essence of who we truly are; our wellspring of

The high Self

unconditional love and an ever-abundant source of complete comfort.

In balance, our low self ascends from nature and encapsulates all of our evolutionary and genetic traits. It is finite; programmed for survival; moves away from pain; coordinates our automatic bodily support systems – such as circulation, respiration and digestion.

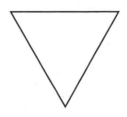

The low self

It operates through instinct and primal emotions; is the home of our ego; and the part of us which forever seeks comfort.

Get the Balance Right

From the moment we are born both our high Self and low self are present within us to varying degrees and, like yin and yang, are intended to work together in a balanced partnership of inter-active harmony.

Our high Self is created to lead. It processes the qualities of imagination and inspiration and shines with a brilliance that illuminates a path for our low self to follow. Our low self is an effective 'doer' and is best suited to managing and organizing repetitive tasks and actions.

When our high Self leads we live with a sense of purpose and passion that not only creates happiness, peace and abundance in our life, but also forms a connection to our inner source of complete comfort.

However, when our low self tries to lead it lacks the qualities of vision and heart, and often becomes lost in chasing external comfort dragons that run down dark and stony paths. When we live from our low self we become overly reactive to our environment and are driven by fear to secure food, shelter and clothing, only afterwards looking beyond for a deeper sense of meaning and purpose.

In contrast, when we *lead* from our high Self, while *managing* the journey from our low self, we seek meaning and purpose first, then, through it, naturally attract and create food, shelter and clothing in abundance.

Trapped in Our Self

While our high Self is fluid and exists in the moment, our low self is grounded and becomes rooted in established beliefs, fixed attitudes and repeated behaviour, all of which contribute to form our sense of personality or self. The more fixed in beliefs and hardened in attitudes our low self becomes, the more it overshadows or blocks the light from our high Self. Our ego becomes dominant, clouds the window on our soul, and we become blind to the best part of us.

> There is an ancient Indian tale about three blind men who encounter an elephant for the first time. One inspects the trunk and concludes the beast is like a big snake. The next finds a leg and decides he is sensing some kind of tree. The third grabs the tail and thinks he is holding a rope.

What's the moral of this story? We all see life from a different perspective depending on our past experience and beliefs, and are all blind in some way, especially about the ultimate truth of our Self.

Fortunately, no matter how thick our ego may become, wise men and women from all cultures and ages have seen through it to the truth shown in the eyes of a newborn, and have known this truth to also exist within their Self and all humanity.

Evolving from Low self to High Self

In ancient times it was believed that *gnosis* – knowledge of the self – was the highest of all wisdoms. Knowing your self – your own beliefs, attitudes and behaviours – helps you to *be* at your best, in all that you *do*, and thereby *have* your best experiences in life, create your best results.

However, if we are blind to our self, unconscious of our own low-self habit-patterns and motivations, then like a drunken fool we repeatedly stumble into the same old pitfalls. While there are many paths in life that can be taken, some less challenging than others, and many that are well meant and spiritually intended, the qualities of the low self and ego are fundamentally the same. The low self is constantly moving away from some form of pain or other, whether real or imagined, in situations and relationships, and therefore never truly finds lasting complete comfort.

For the person who is driven by their low-self ego there is no true rest, they are always on edge in some way, wanting, worrying or warring. There may be great achievements, rewards and accolades, but the real goal of life is not accumulation, conquest or even accomplishment, but rather peace, happiness and complete comfort. No matter what you may attain in life, without peace of mind and an authentic feeling of complete comfort at your core, all else ultimately becomes meaningless.

The Journey Home

The prime purpose of our life, the 'big goal' that we are each born with, is to reunite our low self with our high Self, like two partners reuniting who have grown apart. When we marry our low self with our high Self, we merge our qualities and, through the complementary difference, create 'synergy of self'. We become our true Self.

Courage balanced with consideration, ego balanced by spirit and love balanced by natural fear allow us to be spontaneous and flow in harmony with the current of creation to live in complete comfort, perfect peace and abundance.

By *making the two one*, bringing our high Self and low self together into an integrated true Self, we are able to live our life with spirit, create our chosen desires and know the truth of who we really are. Many people only realize this great truth on their deathbed when their eyes again become as a child's and they are

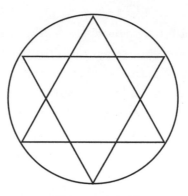

The True Self

able to see beyond the mask of their ego to the pure pristine consciousness from whence they came. It is, however, our divine right and prime purpose to find and live the truth of our Self as early as possible.

Conscious Self-integration, the True Path

Only by bringing our high Self and low self together to become our true Self are we fully empowered for life's journey – able to find meaning in the good as well as the so-called bad; the desired as well as the unintended.

Combining the two into one is humanity's quest, one we have been pursuing since the birth of consciousness. We are gradually moving from the *true nature of humanity*, which is largely fear-driven, ego-based and self-centred, to the *nature of true humanity*, which is purpose-led, heart-centred and selfless.

If life is a journey, then surely the true goal of life is not to reach the journey's end as quickly as possible, nor to collect the most souvenirs. The true goal is to make the most of the trip, having the most fun and creating the most happiness along the way.

This is not the type of happiness that comes just from experiencing happy events, for we will all meet rocks of disappointment, chasms of despair and pools of sorrow along our path.

The happiness that springs from your true Self is totally free and abundant. It is the happiness that is *independent* of happy events. It is the happiness and peace of mind that come from learning to evolve your low self, find your high Self and integrate the two to become your true Self. It's the path that all the great teachers and leaders, sages and shamans, prophets and poets have travelled through the ages, laying down signs as they went that each of us might follow if we choose.

> **The true purpose of life is a warm heart.**
> **THE DALAI LAMA**

The Seven Stages of Self

Shakespeare wrote:

> All the world's a stage,
> And all the men and women merely players:
> They have their exits and their entrances;
> And one man in his time plays many parts,
> His acts being seven ages.
>
> *AS YOU LIKE IT*, II, VII

Stage 1: Making an Entrance

The stage is set, the play has not yet begun, the curtain rises and we emerge from the place of pure pristine consciousness to slip on our costume of matter and begin our part in the great drama of life.

Immediately our low self acts its proper role by playing to our survival needs. Coordinating the stimulation streaming from our senses, it establishes neural pathways defining sight, sound, touch, taste and smell. This is the palette from which we begin to paint the picture of our mind. Gradually our awareness rises, our senses focus and the world around us starts to take shape and substance. It becomes solid and real.

So begins the great task of consciously learning how to survive in the kingdom of matter. Our high Self sets the intention; then, through repetition, all manner of initially complex tasks quickly become an *unconscious action* of our low self, as we learn to feed ourselves, maintain our balance, walk and talk. Once mastered, these skills are taken for granted as automatic habits.

Stage 2: Learning Your Lines

With each experience and subsequent thought we form more and more mental pictures of our *self* as being *separate* from the world around us. Eventually the realization dawns: 'I am an individual.' Our naturally integrated Self divides and the formation of our ego begins.

The word *ego* comes from Latin and means 'I, myself'; for humans in general, this definition extends outwards – 'I': these thoughts; 'I': this body, these possessions, this career. Our ego associates itself with the content of our mind, while our high Self is the awareness observing in the background. The more we identify with the picture in our head, the stronger our ego becomes. It thrives on attachment to things, so along with the magic word 'I' come the connected terms of 'me', 'my' and 'mine'.

'It's mine' and 'I want to do it myself' are two of the most-repeated mantras in early childhood, all acting to further our sense of individualization or self. Separating from the 'we' of collective consciousness and learning to become 'I' is a traumatic experience. Children need the comfort of abundant love to feel secure while exploring, learning and growing.

Unless we are helped to find our balance and connection with our high Self through love, praise and positive reinforcement, our low-self beliefs, attitudes and behaviours become dominant and may be carried through to our adult personality.

Stage 3: Acting the Part

If we are overly compared to others or excessively measured against criteria and social standards it causes our sense of security to come from the outside – how much more or less we think we are in comparison to another person. A child who feels they are worth less than someone else may continue to feel this way in adulthood, developing a continual feeling of worthlessness. This lies at the very core of low self-image and low self-esteem. Sometimes in our discomfort we become introverted – timid and shy; other times extroverted – loud and showy. Both are really a mask to cover over the deep insecurity of feeling 'I'm not good enough.'

The confidence demonstrated in youth is most often the bravado and cockiness of an unbalanced ego, superficially boosted by growing physical strength, chemical changes within the body and the mental accumulation of knowledge which usually surfaces as arrogance and idealism.

However, beneath this mask of false bravery a person whose low self is dominant always feels in some way insecure and needs others to envy their achievements, possessions or looks.

If we are unsure of or blind to our true Self we will be easily influenced by society. The ego craves attention, which results in the need to be popular. When we're introverted this need might be voiced as 'I wish I were like you', and when extroverted, 'You wish you were like me.' Either way, we're not being true to our Self, and instead are only acting the part, desperately putting on a front in an attempt to fit in with what we believe will bring us comfort.

Stage 4: Being on Cue

While pursuing almost any aim or ambition serves in some way to enliven us by bringing focus, motivation and a sense of achievement, goals centred just on having more – more things, grades or accomplishments – tend to be of the ego, and therefore carry with them negative energies. We become predominantly reactive, driven by fear, with our low-self beliefs, attitudes and habits often creating as many tragedies as triumphs in life.

In contrast, by going beyond mere material ambition and committing to a positive sense of purpose or goal that is bigger than our low self, it starts an upward spiral of self-growth leading to the discovery of our true Self. Having a goal that is more than our ego, something that touches another's life, is the turning point on our journey that inspires us to reach for our true greatness. The stronger the sense of purpose we feel the greater we stretch our self – mentally, emotionally and physically – and the more we become as a person.

While there are many types of purpose, such as a vision, a mission or commitment to another, your *prime purpose* is always to evolve your low self towards greater levels of Self. This is the purpose we are all born with. It's encoded into our genes and represents the drive of evolution that whispers from our core, 'Be all you can be.'

Stage 5: Learning to Ad-lib

As you walk the path of your purpose, growing in self-esteem with each step, you begin to glimpse the inner freedom and complete comfort that come from learning to *choose your response* to the various tides and tidings of your life.

Maturity does not automatically come with age; it comes from being clear in your self and therein discovering your Self. Working through our low-self issues, unconsciously accumulated beliefs, attitudes and habits, helps us to realize the truth of our Self, the true you, free from the grip of ego.

Being 'free of ego' doesn't mean not having one; everything must have its opposite if it is to be complete. Beliefs and habits are useful on many levels. Being 'free of ego' means you *consciously choose* those beliefs, attitudes and habits that serve you most, and drop those that don't.

Our greatest freedom can be found in our divine ability to choose our own thoughts. Through exercising our free will we are able to choose our beliefs, attitudes and habits, and through them influence the quality of our life. Learning to choose our thoughts allows us to be truly *response-able* – that is, able to choose our high-Self response to situations our low self would usually react to.

In this way we stop blaming and being *reactive* to life's peaks and troughs, and instead become *present*, consciously choosing a creative response that positively builds up our self, others around us, and our environment.

Choosing your high-Self response helps lift you out of the rut of self-destructive habit-patterns and gradually moves you beyond the cloud of your ego to the light of your true Self.

Stage 6: A Star Performance

The power to choose is a gift that brings with it responsibility, for we are all free to focus on what's best or worst about our self and life. The key to wisdom, demonstrated through response-ability, is *self-selection*. Whichever you focus on, your low self or high Self grows in your awareness and commands your subconscious, attracting universal consciousness towards it. Selecting to focus on your high Self, the great you, helps you be your true Self more often.

In contrast, when we slip into excessively focusing on what's wrong with us and worst in life, we revert to being our low self more often than not and become beast-like in all manner of horrible ways.

Wisdom flows from a balance of knowledge and experience fused through feeling. Developing our self on the inside enhances our experience of life on the outside. This becomes an upward spiral where faith in the external world is mirrored by faith in our self. Likewise learning patience, acceptance and appreciation of our low self, guided by our high Self, builds our self-esteem and leads to these qualities being demonstrated outwardly, setting an example for others around us.

Stage 7: A Leading Light

Enlightenment can manifest for a single moment or endure for a lifetime. We all become enlightened at some point in life, however briefly. The great souls of humanity reached a level of true Self-integration where they remained enlightened from moment to moment, holding the light of their high Self and anchoring it into their low self, so as to become shining beacons.

The seven stages of self represent not only stages of our individual development but also of humanity's continuing evolution. We are each able to move beyond our animal low self, which is governed by instinct and learned behaviour. Individually, every life, no matter how brief, embarks on the journey, and in some way also adds to humanity's collective progress. It is a journey of self-growth, from low-self ego through to high-Self enlightenment, on which we pass through the lessons of life and corresponding stages of self, and find our way back home, to our inner palace of perfect peace and complete comfort.

Seek the truth within your Self
and the truth will set you free.

Self Mapping:
A System for Conscious Self-evolution

Self Mapping is a unique system of ancient wisdom and scientific understanding specifically created to help you make an authentic journey from your self to your Self.

Integrating your low-self beliefs, attitudes and habits with your high-Self ideals, aspirations and character, the system of Self Mapping helps you connect to your high Self, bring peace to your low self and live from your harmonious true Self. It supports you in becoming a genuine human being who speaks with an authentic voice, follows their heart and acts naturally; walking your talk along the path of your purpose towards the direction of your heartfelt dreams.

This person already exists within you now. Self Mapping, simply, lovingly and powerfully, helps him or her to shine through, bringing out the best in your Self, and helping you manifest the best in your life.

How It Works

In creating your own Self Map, through a combination of words and pictures, you draw the threads of your low self and high Self together. By regularly using your Map you gradually accept your low-self limitations, and hold a positive focus on your high-Self qualities, becoming your true Self a little more each day.

The Self Map that you will be guided to create will act like a magnetic mirror reflecting your true Self, helping you stay conscious of who you choose to be, commanding you on a sub-conscious level to move towards your high Self, and attracting from universal consciousness those situations and circumstances that are of your true Self. Using it on a regular basis will help you gain insight into your low self, high Self and life, choose your responses and attitudes and control your actions or behaviours.

How to Use This Book

This book is a series of insights and observations. The truths within it have a self-authenticating quality; realizing them is like remembering something you already knew but had forgotten. Reading this book is a journey that has many stages and there are many routes that can be taken. The steps for Self Mapping are given at the end of each chapter. The last chapter focuses on regular and repeated use of the system so as to live the teaching of being your Self in your life. You can, if you choose, proceed directly to the Self Mapping system and create your Self Map first, or flick through the key points of the philosophy, or take in the complete text. The choice is yours and all will serve.

I heard it said that:

Some teachings are like a bird flying across the sky – it leaves no tracks that can be followed and yet its presence is unmistakeable.

Whether you choose to let the wisdom contained within unfold into your consciousness or consciously commit to it by creating and using a Self Map, I recommend that you keep a journal of your insights, answers or intentions as they surface. You will find that re-reading them will help you discover deeper truths that act as signs guiding you back home to the complete comfort that is your natural state – simply being your Self.

The Path is through your Self, Truth is in your Self and the great Mystery is your Self.

Freeing Questions

Before you read on, take a moment to think about the following questions:

◆ Which have you lived most from: your self or your Self?

◆ Which has brought you your best experience of life: your self or your Self?

◆ Which will most help you live your life for the future: your self or your Self?

— ◆ —

IN ESSENCE

The essence to remember from this chapter is:

Be your true Self and
live in complete comfort.

Part One

Thought

Chapter 1

Self-awareness

Man, Know Thy Self

Of all the wondrous events that have unfolded throughout the course of humanity's existence our greatest moment must surely have been the birth of self-awareness. It is, after all, the beginning of what makes us human.

Self-awareness, or our *ability to think about our own thinking*, means we are each free to question our thoughts, feelings and actions, and if we decide they don't serve us, we can choose to change them for others that do.

Fold your arms right now. Whichever way you've folded them (right tucked into left or left into right) is a habit-pattern – a set way of doing things. However, raise your awareness of this and you can, if you choose, fold them the opposite way. And while at first it may seem a little awkward, within a few times it will soon start to feel normal as you begin to form a new *consciously chosen* habit-pattern.

Although choosing how to fold your arms may seem a bit trivial, it is in fact this inner freedom of being able to 'choose our way' that has enabled humans to be extremely adaptable. It is the first of the keys that enable us to move beyond the low-self animalistic roots that *determine* or control all other species, and evolve our self to higher levels of awareness. We are truly self-determining.

While all of life is 'aware' to some degree, animals do not have the same level of self-awareness as humans and therefore operate from a lower level of consciousness. An elephant, for example, although possessing a large and intelligent brain with a tremendous memory, is limited like other creatures in that once it has been trained or conditioned to behave in a certain way it is unable to *consciously choose* to be different. Elephants that are returned to the wilderness have to be retrained or conditioned into being wild again.

In like manner, it is when we live from our low-self animalistic awareness that we become chained to our habits, even harmful ones, while in truth we really could be free. Our entire lives are run on habit-patterns, and while many of them may feel totally normal because we have lived with them for so long, that does not mean they are necessarily natural or best for us.

As Keith Ellis writes in *Bootstraps*:

> Like the elephant, we are unconscious of our own strength. When it comes to understanding the power we have to make a difference in our own lives, we might as well be asleep. If you want to make your dreams come true, wake up.

The awareness of our low self, like that of all animals, is based on our past. With repeated experience we begin to think a certain way, feel a certain way, act a certain way, and before we know it, we've become *set* in our ways.

Only by raising our awareness and observing our low self from our high Self are we able to see rightly and imagine being different, imagine being another way, imagine being *free*, being our *true Self*.

Of all the creatures in the kingdom of matter, humans alone have been gifted this key of high-Self-awareness. It means we are each free to unlock the shackles of any past conditioning and choose a positive high-Self response over any of our low-self habits, animal instincts or learnt behaviour.

> Know then thyself,
> presume not God
> to scan;
> The proper study of
> Mankind is Man.
> ALEXANDER POPE

Living from our true Self and being self-determining doesn't mean ignoring or denying our natural drives and urges. It simply means we are not *fixed* by them. We are not programmed. We are not determined. We are each free in the deepest, truest sense, and raising our awareness is our master key.

The Keys to the Kingdom

The birth of self-awareness is the birth of humanity, both collectively as a species and individually in each person.

The moment we became self-aware as a species was the moment we became human in the truest sense. In like manner, it's in the moments when we are each individually aware of our high Self, living from the spirit within, that we become truly humane – a genuine human being capable of compassion even in the darkest days of despair.

This higher awareness enables us to empathise. It is the essence of our high Self, the hallmark of our true Self and the nature of our *true humanity*.

Within the course of life everyone will at some point experience moments of enlightenment and connection to their true humanity. Sadly, however, throughout history the true nature of humanity has been that most people are often *unaware* and in the grip of their low-self ego.

Whenever we are 'unaware' collectively or individually, we become disconnected from our empathic, compassionate, spiritually guided high Self. We no longer lead from our heart and instead become driven by fear. It is in these moments of *unconsciousness* that we revert to our low-self animal instincts, which, if unbalanced by an over-inflated ego, become truly *beast-like* in their nature.

At such times humans can descend to being an animal capable of greater savagery, barbarism and brutality than any other creature on the planet. From the atrocities of war and genocide of societies, through to the cruelties inflicted on its own children, humanity has abused itself.

The key to setting us free, as a species or an individual, is to raise our awareness beyond our low-self ego, become connected to our high-Self spirit and merge the two, so as to live from our true Self.

> Success does not depend so much on external help as on self-reliance.
> **ABRAHAM LINCOLN**

Conscious Self-evolution

Our high Self and the energy of unconditional love that it emanates actually run counter-clockwise to the idea of the 'law of the jungle'. This idea cannot explain humanity's extraordinary capacity for compassion. And, while it's clear that we've inherited from our animal ancestors many wondrous and effective low-self survival instincts which protect us well, especially in times of danger, it is unquestionably our high-Self spiritual qualities that have most served humankind's evolution.

It is high-Self qualities such as *empathy* and *peacefulness*, demonstrated through acts of kindness, which lead to tolerance, create understanding and gain cooperation. It's these high-Self qualities of the *heart*, much more than our low-self fear-driven behaviours of the *ego*, that enable communities to form and civilizations to flourish. Such qualities are the glue that brings people together. War is the wedge that drives us apart.

Our understanding of life is created in our mind. Therefore our awareness of our self equals our awareness of ultimate reality. Over the millennia, and from all cultures and corners of the world, the importance of raising awareness and leading your life from your true Self has been realized. Many great teachers of awareness have emerged throughout the centuries with words of wisdom to help others find their way along their path of self-discovery.

In the 1st century the disciple Didymos Judas Thomas recorded:

> If those who guide your Being say to you:
> 'Behold the Kingdom is in heaven,'
> then the birds of the sky will precede you;
> if they say to you: 'it is in the sea,'
> then the fish will precede you.
> But the Kingdom is at your centre
> and is about you.
> When you know your Selves then you will
>   be Known,
> and you will be aware that you are
> the sons of the living Father.
> But if you do not Know yourselves
> then you are in poverty,
> and you are the poverty.

THE GOSPEL OF THOMAS

Part of the original teaching of Christ, as with many Eastern philosophies, was that 'heaven' or 'the Kingdom' was not so much a place as a *way of being*. The gateway to the Kingdom was a state of mind, an attitude of heart and conviction of action, which could be entered into to help us create a heavenly experience right here on earth in our everyday lives and situations.

> I've never been poor, only broke. Being poor is a frame of mind. Being broke is only a temporary situation.
> MIKE TODD

However, if we are unaware of our low self and high Self; if we are blind to our own failings and limitations, as well as ignorant of our inner freedom and the richness of our spirit, then we become 'the poverty' of our own creation – a poverty of outlook and attitude that creates the experience of poverty in our lives, regardless of the level of our wealth or achievement.

The Secret of Success

Choose to raise your awareness and live the experience of heaven, more often than that of hell, and you'll enter the Kingdom of your true Self to live in a state of complete comfort and eternal bliss.

This highest of natural secrets is ultimately discovered by anyone who seeks the truth and raises their awareness of the nature of life and the meaning of true success. It is therefore inscribed within the sacred teachings of many cultures.

In the ancient world the Oracle at Delphi was considered the fountain of wisdom. Philosophers, kings and princes would travel there from far and wide to receive a message of guidance – an *oracle* – from the priestess of Apollo on matters of the greatest importance. On a pillar by the entrance of the temple was inscribed what was considered the highest of all wisdoms: *Gnothi seauton* – 'Know Thyself'.

While civilizations rise and fall, some things never change. Truths of the Self are eternal and fundamental. Some 2,500 years after the temple at Delphi reached its peak, modern university research has discovered that people with high self-awareness are likely to be ideal for management development and for a role in future leadership.

> He who knows others is wise; he who knows himself is enlightened.
> **LAO-TZU**

It would seem that at any age, in any occupation or activity, self-awareness creates effectiveness. The more you genuinely 'know thyself' – your own beliefs, attitudes and habits – the more empowered you are to choose those that most suit the situation you face, bring out the best in you, and as you evolve your self, so your world around you blossoms.

How Do You See It?

Look at any culture or society, even those that are non-materialistic, and you will discover different people achieving different levels of happiness, peace and abundance. What determines all of these different levels of success is not really the start we each receive in life, *it is the awareness we develop as we pass through it.* And the people who achieve the true success of living joyfully have a very different level of awareness from those that don't.

> The pessimist sees difficulty in every opportunity. The optimist sees the opportunity in every difficulty.
> **WINSTON CHURCHILL**

The happiest of people don't necessarily have the best of everything; they simply choose to see the best in everything, and through it find complete comfort.

There are many aspects or forms of awareness that help us function in life, such as an awareness of our environment, which determines our effectiveness at moulding it to our desires. For example, the awareness of the Kalahari Bushmen enables them to flourish in an environment where others would see only desolation. Likewise, the awareness of a New York businessperson helps him or her to prosper in an environment that would appear bewildering to the tribesmen.

Similarly, an awareness of others, being able to empathize, understanding that different people have different viewpoints, beliefs, attitudes and habits, helps us to get along with others in harmony, and through celebrating diversity, create great synergies.

However, above all else, it is awareness of our self and Self, knowing the outlooks, attitudes and habits of our low self, while having a high-Self sense of purpose and meaning for our life, that has most helped humanity to flourish.

The more we raise our awareness of our high Self, and focus on what is best in us and our life, the more inspired we become and motivated into action, even in the most challenging of situations. In Milton's words:

> ... he who reigns within himself, and rules
> Passions, desires, and fears is more [than] a king.

What Mask?

While awareness is representative of light, life and love, a lack of awareness often results in darkness, decay and death.

The opposite of being self-aware is to be self-deluded, ignorant or oblivious to the truth. Sometimes we experience delusions of grandeur – thinking we are superior to others – and at other times we suffer feelings of inferiority, when we are unaware of our own hidden potential and innate worth. In either case we cannot see the glory of our true Self, blinded as we are by the shadow of our low-self ego. The more we sink into our ego the more we lose sight of what brings us true comfort. Like a mask, our ego not only blocks others from seeing who we truly are, but also distorts the light we receive from others and our high Self.

There are talent shows around the world where people who have little or no talent at all are totally shocked when the judges tell them how awful their performance was. Part of the nervous laughter that comes from the audience is to cover their embarrassment at being able to see what these contestants are clearly *unaware* of in their self: that they really can't sing, dance or act.

At the opposite end of the spectrum, but just as challenged in their own way, are those with real talent who are totally oblivious to it. These people are often overcome by feelings of inferiority and insecurity, which in turn affects their performance. Of course, it is in those rare moments when we are simply being natural, aware and comfortable with who we truly are that we can sing and live with heart and soul, giving our best in every area and aspect of our life.

Who Am I?

Years ago I always laughed when I heard people say they were going off to 'find themselves'. 'How strange', I would scoff. 'I know exactly who I am.' In reality, of course, I was completely ignorant of the truth about my self and Self. Unaware of my own high-Self spirit, I was living a low-self lie and had been blinded by the illusion.

I was playing a game called 'let's pretend' and the rules of the game are that you have to pretend that you're not pretending. Almost everyone plays the game to some extent and in some way. It's the game of putting on masks for the outside world while inwardly feeling very different. 'I'm fine' is seldom the reality for us even though it's the most common answer to 'How are you?'

I wore the mask of 'fine-ness' even though deep down I felt real sadness. I pretended to be confident even though I was actually quite desperately insecure and unsure of myself. I pretended so well, for so long, that I fooled myself into believing my pretence was real. I also fooled a lot of other people along the way, although some saw through the facade.

On the surface I was full of bravado and cockiness, while underneath were deep feelings of uncertainty and insecurity. Because this truth was too painful to look at and acknowledge, I was completely blind to it.

Of course my experience is not unique. Most people are unaware to some degree about the truth of their self. Sometimes it shows up in the little things, like the delegate who sat through my entire workshop picking his nose, totally oblivious to his behaviour. At other times it's the big things, like the way we treat others who we profess to love but who we are actually very cruel to.

Generally, the more unaware of our self we become the more reactive we are to life's ups and downs, experiencing a rollercoaster ride of highs and lows as we react to the triumphs and tribulations of existence. When we wear the mask of ego we become the puppet of our situation, with life constantly pulling our strings.

What a pity we cannot see that which is before our own eyes, that we, the rightful heirs of God's good grace, do not find the treasure that is ours.

Living in Low-self Hell

The deeper we descend into our low self the thicker the mask of our ego grows and the more unconscious and reactive we become. Each fall from awareness sees us slip further into our low self and revert to being beast-like in some way. Driven by distorted survival instincts we become increasingly low-self-centred or selfish. This aspect of our animalistic past is not negative in itself until it becomes unbalanced by an over-inflated ego. When this happens the need that drives us isn't really food, shelter or clothing, but the ego's need to feel important, to feel superior in some way, which creates a whole range of destructive ways of being such as pride, vanity, lust and greed, spiralling all the way down to prejudice, intolerance, resentment and persecution.

Conflicts usually bring out the worst in humanity; people go into low-self survival mode but, driven by a fearful ego, become excessive in their response. From the horrors of war through to the battle of relationships and the daily struggle that many people experience just to get through life, in all situations of uncertainty or conflict we wear our masks to protect us while doing battle – in the office, at the supermarket or even in our own home.

> The meaning of things lies not in the things themselves but in our attitude towards them.
> **ANTOINE DE SAINT-EXUPÉRY**

We believe our masks shield us but, in truth, they actually block us from seeing the splendidness of our true Self, the glory of life and reality of our situations. Often people become so accustomed to wearing and justifying their mask that they grow oblivious to it, not because it fits particularly well but because they've become desensitized from carrying it for so long.

Shifting Awareness – Transforming Realities

The path of life and society progresses, or evolves, from ignorant to aware, barbaric to civilized, dictator to democracy, determined to self-determined.

Evolution, whether of society, the mind or matter, is not an even, unified process but rather a slow gradual build-up that, when a 'critical-mass point' is reached, suddenly grows experientially to settle at a new higher level of order and complexity, ready to begin the process or growth over again.

The more we raise our awareness of the workings of the external world, the causes and effects of creation, the more links we form between brain cells in our internal world. It is through this process of connecting brain cells that we form, hold and develop ideas. The more brain cells we link together the more we establish beliefs and outlooks. These in turn form 'patterns of understanding' that we project on to the world around us like mental scaffolding, propping up our opinions and perceptions.

Life is a great teacher and every once in a while we will experience something – shocking or blissful – that tears down all our scaffolding, causes us to stop pretending, be still, take stock, and ask deep and searching questions. It is in these moments that we often gain new insights, making or breaking a major brain-cell connection, which (like reaching a critical-mass point) triggers whole structures of brain-cell connections to spontaneously reorganize themselves into higher levels of meaning and understanding. This shift in awareness, known as a 'paradigm shift' can cause us to see our self and life in a completely different light.

In ancient times this same process of changing your outlook was described by the Greek word *metanoia* meaning 'to rethink' or 'seeing with new eyes'.

Everyone will experience paradigm shifts that afterwards affect their outlook, attitude and behaviour. Sometimes they're huge, like my friend who was pronounced clinically dead before being resuscitated. Sometimes they are less so, like the experience of watching your self on video and realizing something about your self you were previously blind to.

However, we don't have to wait for an epiphany in order to gain insight. By consciously shifting our awareness from low self to high Self, negative to positive, we literally alter our brain-cell connections. This not only causes us to see things differently, it also triggers the release of different chemicals into our system which give us different *feelings* and in turn influence us to *behave* in different ways. Ultimately this creates for us a different *experience* of life.

> *Shift your awareness to your true Self and you completely transform your experience of reality.*

Bella Vista

Some years ago while on holiday in India, I visited a remote area and was encouraged by a local man to climb a small mountain that had a temple near the summit. On reaching our goal we settled down to take in the splendid sight. The sunset glowed a glorious orange on the horizon, the valley and villages below were streaked in a thin blanket of mist, a troop of monkeys sat just a few metres away on some old ruins, and multicoloured parrots flew above our heads. 'Beautiful', I gasped, quite overcome by the view. 'Yes', said my friend, who was sitting next to me. 'Shame about that telegraph pole down there though.' I had to strain my eyes to find the telegraph pole, which to me was the equivalent of a needle in a haystack, but it stood out for my friend like a sore thumb.

You've got to look with better eyes than that to see the beauty of life. Some people have an awareness that always makes them notice what's wrong: with their self, people and the world, and often, like my friend, they just can't seem to see past it. Other people see things very differently.

A different point of view is simply a view from a point where you're not, but it doesn't mean physically moving, because you carry your outlooks everywhere that you go. Instead, it requires a shift in your mind.

Recently, while I sat on the garden patio writing, I was joined by my five-year-old daughter, Shanti. I've often found her simple childlike wisdom to be enlightening. When I asked her opinion on viewpoints she replied: 'Daddy, a good view is when you can see the whole of the garden and it looks beautiful. A bad view is when the garden looks nasty. A good view of people means there are patterns all around them. A bad view of people means the patterns are not very nice. There are good people everywhere, but we don't always see them.'

More people than ever before, from all over the world, and in every walk of life, are raising their awareness to higher levels and becoming part of a new universal paradigm. Living from their true Self, they carry a positive outlook that is projected on to everything they observe. They have a level of awareness that sees beyond the surface opinions and dramas of life to the truth of their Self and the natural principles of success that govern the process of creation. They're aware that they can create their own reality, that everything has a meaning and purpose. They see change as opportunity, failure as learning, and choose their response, believing that genuine abundance exists within all.

Deepak Chopra is one of these people and says of this outlook:

> One thing we can do is make the choice to view the
> world in a healthy way. We can choose to see the world
> as safe with only moments of danger rather than seeing
> the world as dangerous with only moments of safety.

See the good in your self that you truly desire. As we raise our awareness of our low self and high Self so we evolve towards enlightenment and become the observer of, instead of part of, our ego. We see beyond it to our true Self – our genuine and authentic Self, and thereby become the conscious creator of our heartfelt desires.

The Self Mapping System

The Self Mapping system is designed to help you be your true Self, your best you, in outlook, attitude and action, as often as possible, so as to make your best choices, experience your best feelings and live your best life.

Becoming your true Self is a journey of integrating the ego of your low-self with the spirit of your high-Self. The Self Mapping system was created to help accelerate your journey by guiding you through a process of mapping your low self and high Self in outlook, attitude and habit, covering six major life areas – mental, emotional, physical, material, social and spiritual, and thereby bringing them all together into one integrated balanced whole, or true Self.

— ◆ —

IN ESSENCE

The essence to remember and live from in this chapter is:

Raise your awareness
of your self and Self
and all else will be
added to you.

Creating Your Self Map

To create your Self Map you will require two Self Mapping templates, one for your high Self and another for your low self. You can copy these from the Appendix of this book, or download them free from www.selfmapping.co.uk and (ideally) print them out on white card. You will also require a pencil, rubber and some coloured pens.

Creating your Self Map can happen in a single hour-long session, or be spread over many sessions and several days. It is strongly recommended that for your first Map you follow each step as it is presented to you at the end of each chapter. This will allow you to capture valuable insights as they come to you and while they are still fresh in your mind. This makes it much easier to create your Map rather than trying to recall them all in one sitting. Likewise, you can update your Map by gradually adding new insights as and when they come to you. Once completed, your Self Map will serve you for many years to come.

To move beyond the grip of our ego we must raise our awareness of its ways so as to loosen its hold upon us. Ask yourself the freeing questions below and then follow the first step to capturing your insights in a Self Map.

- ◆ What are you unaware of in your low self that others can perhaps see?

- ◆ What is your awareness of life? Do you see the telegraph pole or the view?

- ◆ What are you most aware of in others: their darkness or their light?

Step 1 – Low-self Habits

The first step in becoming our true Self is to raise awareness of our low self. In this way we become the observer of, instead of part of, our ego. Seeing past our ego loosens its grip upon us, and we begin an upward spiral towards our true Self, home to our inner place of perfect peace and complete comfort.

Accelerate your journey now by choosing a moment from your past, whether recent or distant, which typifies you living from your low self or ego. Without judging your self, simply observe, as if you were viewing a movie, who you were being in that low moment.

This is an intuitive exercise, so please believe that your subconscious is working with you and consider your first thoughts.

Mental Habits

As you observe your low-self moment, take note of your strongest mental habit. How do you behave mentally? For example, do you have the habit of switching off, ignoring, giving in, running away or distracting yourself from life with TV, exercise or games? Are you closed to other people's points of view and do you need to be right? Do you fall into the habit of boasting, or perhaps arguing for no good reason?

Do not look for the right answer, or indeed make your self wrong in any way; simply raise your awareness of who you are in that low moment and be honest with your self.

If you are stuck, consider the freeing questions on page 34.

Don't allow your ego to stall you through procrastination. Write something, even if you're not totally sure. You can always change it later if a greater insight comes.

Using pencil, so as to be erased later, write what you believe is your main low-self mental habit, in the same way as

Step 1.1

you would say it, but worded in the past tense. For example, rather than writing 'I *am* closed', write 'I've *been* closed.' Place it in the top-right outer triangle of your Self Map mandala as in the example above.

Emotional Habits

Now consider the next area, the emotional. What is your dominant emotional habit when being your low self? For instance, do you mainly act aggressively or submissively? Do you have the habit of losing your temper and shouting, or do you go off and sulk? Perhaps you're controlling and like to play mood-games or become a guilt-tripper so as to get your own way?

Please remember, don't judge yourself, simply observe and record your awareness in the next triangle round in the past tense, like the example opposite.

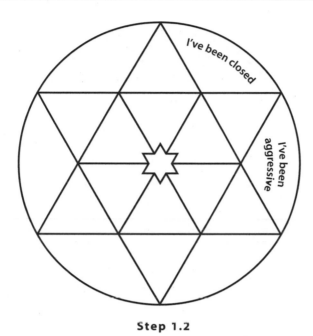

Step 1.2

Physical Habits

Next, observe your habits in the physical area of your life. When being your low self are you physically lazy, clumsy, awkward, stiff, rigid, jittery, tense or stressed? Do you crave, binge or overindulge and physically abuse your self with excessive food, drink, sex or drugs?

Once again, please observe your self without judgement and place your insight, using pencil and the past tense, in the next outer triangle round.

Material Habits

The next area represents the material and financial aspects of your self. What are your low-self habits and behaviour with regard to wealth and prosperity? When low, do you act greedy, scheming, grasping and controlling? Or are you flippant, careless, impulsive, irresponsible and wasteful?

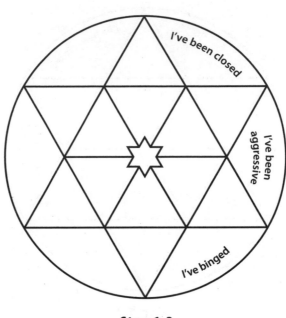

Step 1.3

Once again, connect with a low-self moment and go with the first thought that comes, trusting your intuition. If you feel stuck, consider the freeing questions earlier. Then, as before, capture your insight, writing lightly in pencil in the next triangle round.

Social Habits

Now consider the social aspect of your self and life: how do you show up in your relationships when being your low self? Is your habit to spy, cheat, control, ignore, undermine or bully? Do you act shy or showy? Do you shout, scream, blame or abuse? Again capture your insight without judgement, writing in pencil and worded in the past tense.

Step 1.4

Spiritual Habits

And finally, to complete the outer circle, observe your dominant low-self habits in the spiritual area of your life. When being your low self do you lose all sense of meaning and purpose? Do you go off track? Act in opposition to your own beliefs and values? Become false or bigoted?

Remember there are no right or wrong, good or bad answers. Simply observe your behaviour and record your dominant habit, written in pencil and worded in past tense, as per the example.

Well done! You have now taken the first step in creating your Self Map and ultimately moving beyond your low-self ego.

Chapter 2

Self-belief

I Believe

It has been said that 'manners maketh man'. Some people hold that clothes make the man. In truth, it is belief that makes the man. Our beliefs make us who we are – as in our character traits, personality and ways of being. In turn, who we *are*, shapes what we *do* and thereby the likely outcomes we each *create*.

> Man is made by his belief. As he believes, so is he.
> **BHAGAVAD GITA**
>
> It will be done just as you believed it would.
> **MATTHEW 8:13**

Since the birth of awareness mankind's ability to think about thinking means that humans have always lived by their own beliefs. All ancient creation myths are in essence beliefs about the birth of reality. And from around the world great teachers have shared their beliefs on life and how to live it well. Religion, philosophy and even science all ultimately rest on people's beliefs.

Beliefs draw people together and also drive them apart. In fact, so incredibly powerful are our beliefs that throughout the ages, just as today, people have not only lived by them, a very great many are also prepared to die for them.

Whether you are aware or not of your personal beliefs they will ultimately influence your entire life – from the level of your education through to the career you pursue; the people and opportunities you attract; if and who you marry; your state of health and wealth, mentally, emotionally and physically; your sense of faith and belonging or indeed not having a sense of faith or belonging. On an everyday basis, your beliefs govern the type of life you live, how you conduct your self through it, and whether or not you find true and lasting comfort.

In essence, you are your beliefs. And they not only make you who you are, they also shape and create your life.

Painting a Picture of Reality

Each belief that we fix in our mind is like a dab of paint that adds to the stained-glass window of our perception and thereby colours our awareness.

Beliefs are our filters on reality. Every belief that we hold acts as a blueprint or template of what we've already decided is right or wrong, good or bad, true or false. Like a personal compass our beliefs help us to navigate through the endless and often repetitive decisions of life. Without them we would need to constantly and consciously re-evaluate every twist, turn and fork in our path, which would be overwhelming to the point of insanity.

Each of our beliefs in effect says, 'This is the way it is, the way you are, the way life works; you don't need to think it all through again.' They are the operating instructions for how we believe we should be and it's generally accepted by psychologists that:

Your level of performance will never be significantly higher than your beliefs about your ability.

Self-regulated

Your low self acts like an autopilot; it is the regulator; its job is to help you stay on course. Your beliefs are like the detail of your mental-map that the regulator checks to keep you the same each day. The system works well and allows us to travel through life without constant conscious effort. The great challenge is that we not only form beliefs that support us and empower our life – we also carry a great many others that limit us, dampen our spirits and stifle our talents. Like a bad map, they mislead us and we become lost. Often, we will have one set of beliefs that moves us a step forward, while another set moves us a step, or sometimes two, back.

> **Whether you believe you can or whether you believe you can't – you're right.**
> **HENRY FORD**

Life is a self-fulfilling prophecy and your beliefs are the soothsayer. They are the constant commands to your subconscious about how you should *be*, what you should *do* and the results you should *have*.

The Good News

The great news is that we are each blessed with a special gift, a great treasure, our divinity, you could say. We each carry the key of self-awareness and are therefore free to question our beliefs and choose new ones if we please. Regardless of environment, past experience, upbringing or genetic inheritance, we each have the power to achieve this highest of all successes because we are each mentally free and can choose our thoughts.

Your beliefs about your self, society or reality, are simply thoughts that you've accepted as true. At any time, you can choose to think a different thought, about your self or life, and thereby create a new belief – a new map by which to live your life.

Highs and Lows

A belief, being something you've decided is true, is not held in your conscious questioning mind, it instead sits in your subconscious accepting mind. Most people are generally unaware of their deeper beliefs and motivations. However, begin to question your self, your opinions, attitudes and actions, and you will start to discover that you have beliefs for every aspect and area of your self and life. Generally, they will fall into two basic categories: those of your high Self and those of your low self.

Low-self beliefs, being of the earth, are most often founded and grounded in physical experience. They say: 'Life happens – the sun rises, the moon glows, the wind blows. I know it because I've experienced it.'

In contrast, high-Self beliefs, being of the spirit within, move beyond mere physical experience and into the realm of positive expectation, hope or faith. High-Self beliefs, or belief in the Self, equate to: 'I am free to create my own life – shine my own light, choose my own path, define my own meaning, and ride the winds of change towards my heartfelt desires.'

High-Self beliefs focus on the future and are centred on 'I can', whereas low-self-beliefs are most often stuck in the past and fixated on 'I can't.' The high Self believes, while the low self doubts.

Some 'I can't' beliefs are genuinely helpful. For instance, 'I can't jump off the roof without risk of injury', serves us well. The challenge comes when we try to lead our life from our low-self beliefs because they are governed by past experience, which translates into: 'I can't jump any higher than I've jumped before.' Or worse still, 'I can't jump.'

Beliefs such as these, focused on the self's limitations, really don't serve at all. If allowed to become dominant, they can actually block us from reaching our true potential and finding complete comfort.

Within my work I regularly meet people who have great abilities, but little or no belief in their Self. This severely restricts the use of their skills and knowledge. When their self-doubt takes hold they become nervy, stiff with fear and find it hard to bring forth the great talent they possess.

Self-belief is like a valve that turns on the flow of our talent, skills and knowledge. Self-doubt turns it all back off again.

Keeping the Faith

High-Self beliefs and low-self beliefs differ not only in focus but also in substance. While beliefs of the high Self can be supported by experiences from our past, ultimately they rest on faith because genuine Self-belief asks that you believe when there is no proof, no past experience to assure you.

> I tell you the truth, if you have faith as small as a mustard seed, you can say to this mountain, 'Move from here to there' and it will move.
>
> **MATTHEW 17:20**

Instead of believing just because you have had an experience or observation of life, now you must believe *first* in order to consciously create the life-experience or outcome you desire. Finding faith in your Self enables you to move mountains in your life.

It is faith or belief in our Self – living from our high-Self optimism – that underpins every great achievement of humanity. Having faith in our Self allows us to have faith in the external world and be faithful to our chosen promises, people, purpose and plans.

Without high-Self belief, hope or faith our low-self doubts would limit our thinking to: 'If I couldn't do it before, it means I can't do it now, and there's no point even trying in the future.' We would become controlled by our environment and random experiences, rather than working in harmony with our environment to create our chosen experiences.

Faith is belief in things hoped for, in things not yet experienced. Faith is like magical fairy-dust that you sprinkle wherever you go. Faith is the key to conscious creation and enlightened self-evolution.

Building Self-belief

The creation of Self-belief, the deep-down know-ingness that you are able to consciously cause an effect in your life, begins early in infancy.

Children quickly learn that crying brings an adult, shaking the rattle makes a noise, kicking the cot creates a movement and banging the bowl makes a mess. Linking cause and effect in this way is vital for children to learn that they can influence their own life.

When we enter the world it is with an undeveloped picture of reality, a blank canvas to work on, and from birth we start painting a mental picture of our external environment. It begins with our *experiences*, which cause us to *question*, and result in us placing some form of *meaning* on our experience: whether it was comfort or discomfort, good or bad; whether we should move towards it or avoid it.

Thinking about our experience triggers our brain to release chemicals, such as serotonin and cortisone, into our system. These chemicals create feelings like happiness and sadness

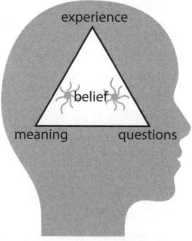

Brain cells and belief

which in turn influence our attitudes and actions. Our actions then cause numerous effects, one of which is more thoughts, and around the cycle we go again.

Each thought-cycle begins as an impulse in a brain cell that travels out along dendrite-arms making connections with other brain cells. Some repeated thoughts become established into neural pathways as we realize that doing *this* results in *that*.

In this way, each external cause and effect that we observe (for example, 'Father Christmas brings toys') is mirrored by forming an internal link between our brain cells, thereby establishing a belief.

Repeated firing of the same brain cells results in continued wiring and the belief grows stronger – from an opinion, to a feeling of certainty and on to an unshakable conviction. Unless, of course, you raise your awareness and link a new cause and effect ('Actually, Mummy and Daddy fetched the toys'), which forms a new and evolved belief.

Being human is one life-long journey of discovery
and ever-evolving beliefs about the gift of life
and how to live it.

Developing the Picture

We each have over 100 billion brain cells, each forming as many as 20,000 dendrite connections. The number of possible thought-patterns, outlooks or beliefs we can each create is mind-boggling.

Imagine that each brain-cell connection or belief you hold is like a pixel of a TV screen showing a picture of reality. The more connections you link, the more beliefs you form, the more pixels you activate, the more detailed, vivid, bright and sharp your picture becomes.

However, at birth, the connections are comparatively few and your picture of reality is little more than a fuzzy blur. An undeveloped picture means that children enter the world with a completely open mind. We are all born with high-Self 'possibility consciousness' and a child's attitude is preset to: 'I don't know what I can do so I'm going to find out.'

Openness is the natural state of mind of our high Self, while our low self is closed because it believes it already knows. Children automatically lead from the qualities of their high Self long before they have experiences and begin to develop low-self limitations.

The high Self and low self work through different sides of the brain. The high Self works primarily with the right hemisphere of our brain. This is the side of our brain that has the gift of imagination and vision. It thinks in pictures and processes our experiences through emotion.

The low self is connected to the left hemisphere. It is the side of our brain that we use for planning and prioritizing. It learns to think in words and processes experiences through logic. The high Self naturally leads, while the low self follows. Try teaching a small child the strategy of putting the straight-edged pieces together when doing a jigsaw and you'll quickly realize that at a young age it's all about the pictures.

At three my daughter Shanti could tell me what the safety instructions picture card found in the back of aeroplane seats meant. As she put it: 'To know what you can do when there is a fire.

'Once upon a time, Daddy, there was an aeroplane. And a blue man put his suitcases in a wardrobe and the lady said, "Everyone get out there's a fire", and they all had a turn on the blow-up slide, and lived happily ever after.'

As a species, just as individuals, humans learn to think and communicate through pictures first, before moving on to words. Although the high Self, operating through the right brain, continues to think in pictures throughout life, the low self, functioning through the left brain, increasingly learns to think in words. It is more often used, and usually grows to become dominant, even to the extent of blocking the light from our high Self's pictures altogether.

Self-creation

While our high Self is fluid and its thoughts are fleeting, our low self is grounded and its repeated thoughts gradually become fixed into beliefs; repeated emotions solidify into attitudes; and repeated actions become set into habits, each contributing to the formation of our self, or personality.

Gradually, as we form more and more beliefs, our sense of self – what we like and dislike – grows and our low self automatically moves us towards the things we believe to be comforting, and away from those we believe are painful.

Holding the right beliefs, the right mental map for our subconscious to follow, is vital if we are to find our way back home to our true Self and complete comfort.

Self-balancing

Our high Self and low self are like flip sides of a coin, the yin and the yang, negative and positive. You can't have one without the other. While the low self doubts, our high Self believes. The low self looks backwards through past experience, while the high Self looks forward through the gift of imagination. The high Self moves towards comfort, the low self is driven by fear to move away from pain.

Both sets of qualities are essential for our well-being. No aspect of the low self is truly negative when in natural balance with the high Self. Fear protects us, past experience informs us and doubt enables us to be discerning.

The low self can only cause damage when we are unbalanced, when self-doubt can spiral into a crisis of confidence, sometimes ending in self-sabotage. Many things can cause people to become unbalanced. Life is often a struggle, particularly in youth. Babies usually experience more discomfort than comfort, cry more than they laugh. A self-limiting belief picked up early in childhood can stick to someone their entire life, subtly holding them back and dragging them down, without their consciously knowing it.

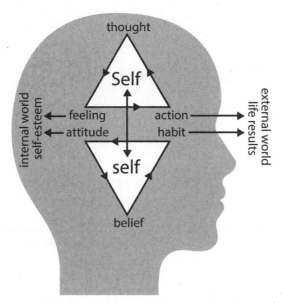

The thought-belief cycles

A friend of mine, who was separated from his mother when he was young, developed the unconscious belief that *the significant woman in his life would always abandon him*. And although he had experienced such abandonment as a five-year-old, the belief continued to *cause an effect* in his adulthood. He would unwittingly drive loyal and faithful partners away while attracting, and being attracted to, partners who were unsuitable and who would invariably leave him.

This is only one example of a subconscious self-limiting belief that we can pick up, operate from and perhaps even pass on to our own children. In some ways, it's like karma.

Some other common low-self beliefs and attitudes are:

◆ I'm stupid.

◆ I can't help it.

◆ I'm unattractive.

◆ I'm not good enough.

◆ Life happens by accident.

◆ There's nothing I can do about it.

Well-meaning parents, teachers, friends, the media, social groups and religions can all have a tremendous impact on us with *their* beliefs, *their* attitudes and *their* behaviours.

For instance, think about how it feels to hear things like, 'Why do you always get it wrong?' or 'You're so messy, clumsy, wasteful…'

Such things may be said without any real malice, but if they are heard regularly, the *comment* becomes the *command*. Hearing again and again, 'You're so messy', creates a picture in the child's head of their being that way, which eventually becomes a belief and thereby a subconscious command to *make it so*.

Sometimes we simply experience limiting beliefs through the attitudes of a significant other, such as a parent. The most common such beliefs revolve around work and money: 'Oh we're not the type of people that do those things, live that way, get that job, or go to university. You have to work hard to get anywhere. You've got to have money to make money; it's dirty, unspiritual, the root of all evil. There's not enough for everyone. You've got to fight to get your share. You can't have your cake and eat it.' Or the really cheery, 'Life's a bitch and then you die.'

Beliefs such as these result in poor attitudes and create a dire reality that limits our growth and positive experience of life. And while we will all pick up some limiting low-self beliefs, we are each also blessed with the high-Self freedom to raise our awareness and move beyond them. For life to be lived well, in heart, mind, body and soul, it must be lived from the high Self, the visionary spirit within that is the natural leader for our low self to harmoniously support and follow. Together they create a truly authentic, synergistic partnership – our true Self.

Be Open

The process of maturity and wisdom, of moving from your low self to your high Self, is not a matter of age, knowledge or skills, but rather *clarity of belief*. Being fluid of mind not fixed. Understanding that your beliefs are *your* beliefs. They are *your* truth. That does not mean they are necessarily *the* truth.

William Blake put it beautifully:

> This Life's dim Windows of the Soul
> Distorts the Heavens from Pole to Pole
> And leads you to Believe a Lie
> When you see with, not thro', the Eye.

No matter how sure we may be about the correctness of our beliefs, they are only ever our interpretation of reality. The truth, the world around us, reality, is often far beyond our level of awareness. What we believe to be true is often just a level of truth – a slice of understanding in the magical never-ending layer-cake of reality.

If two people sit in the same room, one might say it is hot while the other thinks it cold. The actual temperature of the room is the *truth* – reality. Each person's opinion of whether it is hot or cold is their truth – their *personal* reality.

We each live a slightly different and unique reality because we each hold a slightly different and unique set of beliefs, *our truth* as we see it.

*Seek the truth in your Self and the truth
will set you free.*

Hear the Buddha's words of wisdom on this subject:

> Do not believe in anything simply because you have heard it. Do not believe in anything simply because it is spoken and rumoured by many. Do not believe in anything simply because it is found written in your religious books. Do not believe in anything merely on the authority of your teachers and elders. Do not believe in traditions because they have been handed down for many generations. But after observation and analysis, when you find that anything agrees with reason and is conducive to the good and benefit of one and all, then accept it and live up to it.

As Far as We Know

Throughout the course of history the collective view of reality has shifted many times. Our senses tell us the world is flat, and for the longest time this was 'the truth' or *collective view*; until awareness shifted, beliefs changed and it was discovered to be round.

> You create your own universe as you go along.
> **WINSTON CHURCHILL**

Another popular belief was that the Earth was at the centre of the universe, the stars revolving around it, until the sight from a telescope showed it to be otherwise. And that matter had substance went without question for the majority of people until scientists discovered it was mostly empty space.

In each age people have stated what they believed was 'the truth' only to see it dissolved or developed by the next generation who discover another layer in the cake of reality. The all-important missing line from most scientific reports is: 'as far as we know'.

Reality is always changing. Quantum physicists only calculate in terms of probability because a particle can exist in many positions or super-positions at the same time. In fact science is now discovering what many ancient teachings have always maintained: that ultimately reality is an illusion.

It Matters What You Mind

It is believed that at birth and in our early days, before our fundamental brain-cell connections have been fully established, we experience reality in our mind as just pure vibrating energy. This is exactly how many scientists describe the essence of all matter: as pure energy. Or, as Sir James Jeans states:

> The annihilation of matter is merely unbottling imprisoned wave energy, and setting it free to travel through space.

As far as we know, physical reality is over 99 per cent empty space, and even the bit that's not is a fluctuation of energy and intelligence flashing into and out of existence.

The leading scientific theories, or beliefs, that explain this at a subatomic level suggest that all reality is like a net of energy created from tiny 'strings' that when disturbed or plucked vibrate and produce matter. Different rates of vibration create different types of matter. And the whole universe is a symphony of interacting vibrations all playing together in harmony to produce life.

You are part of reality. You are over 99 per cent empty space. That means you are flashing into and out of existence, giving off vibrations, creating attractions and playing your part in the orchestra.

Each thought you think produces an energy that creates a vibration, like plucking a string. A repeated thought which becomes a *belief* is a constant strumming. Through our thoughts, words and deeds we not only add music to the great song of life, we can also ride the rhythm to create our own tune.

Strumming the Strings of Life

The prime law of creation for science or religion is cause and effect, known in some traditions as karma, and described in the Bible in terms of harvest:

> Whatsoever a man soweth, that shall he also reap.
>
> GALATIANS 6:7

Buddhists believe likewise:

> ...for every event that occurs, there will follow another event whose existence was caused by the first, and that, this second event will be pleasant or unpleasant based on the skilfulness of the act which caused it.

When we apply the universal law of cause and effect to the self it shows that while actions or deeds shape the course of life, it is in turn our attitudes that influence our actions, and if we follow the chain back, the ultimate cause is thought.

Thought is the first creation, and on an energy level, your thoughts are reality. The strength of your belief determines how quickly you bring them into being. Drawing your dreams into physical reality requires consistency of intention, or belief – a constant command to your subconscious and the universe about your life and how you choose to be within it.

Our beliefs not only influence our perception, attitudes and actions, causing us to see the darkness or the light, but also set up a whole range of vibrations that attract and create situations and substance of like vibration.

Each of our thoughts, negative or positive, triggers chemicals which create feelings and together encode the cells of our body with lingering vibrations of attraction or repulsion. Like batteries, our

> The spirit of a person's life is ever shedding some power, just as a flower is steadily bestowing fragrance upon the air.
>
> THOMAS STARR KING

beliefs radiate energy, drawing to us, or repelling, peace, people and prosperity.

When I first learnt of the philosophy of positive thinking, like most people I had only a surface layer of optimism under which sat a deep pool of negativity. I thought fleetingly about what I wanted and thereby created an attraction for those things. However, I was also carrying a contradictory negative belief, which produced an energy of repulsion that cancelled out my positive intention.

> You can have anything you want if you will give up the belief that you can't have it.
> **DR ROBERT ANTHONY**

The universe, like your subconscious, does not make judgements about the thoughts you hold and the energy you transmit, it simply responds to your commands.

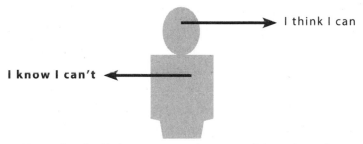

I think I can

I know I can't

Negative beliefs can cancel out positive thoughts

Low-self beliefs, focused on scarcity, lack and limitation, drive us in one direction while our positive high-Self intentions draw us in another. The result is that we often end up pulling our self apart; building our life up only to subconsciously tear it all back down again.

— ◆ —

IN ESSENCE

The essence to remember and live from in this chapter is:

You become your dominant belief about your self or Self.

Creating Your Self Map

Before engaging in the second step of the Self Mapping system, ask your self these freeing questions:

◆ What is your dominant belief about your self?

◆ What is your dominant belief about your life?

◆ What is your dominant belief about reality?

Step 2 – Low-self Attitudes

If you have completed Step 1 you will have captured a snapshot of your low-self habits – how you regularly act or behave when low in the main areas of your life.

> Know what is within your sight, and what is hidden from you will become clear. For there is nothing hidden that will not be revealed.
>
> **THE GOSPEL OF THOMAS**

If you haven't yet finished filling in all the outer spaces, perhaps because you feel blocked or unsure, simply continue with this step. It will help you gain greater clarity and you can always go back and complete any unfinished statements later.

Now, get back in touch with a low-self moment from your past, either one you have already thought about in the last step or another. Remember to view your self without judgement, as if you were watching a movie. As you reconnect with the moment, notice *who you were being*, this time thinking about your attitudes.

Mental Attitudes

As before, trust your intuition, and beginning with the mental, observe your dominant attitude when being your low self. Have you been stubborn, defeatist, impatient or unfocused?

Step 2.1

Consider what you have already stated as your habit, and think about what attitude may sit behind it. For example, if you have stated 'I've been closed' as your habit then maybe the attitude behind it is arrogance or stubbornness.

Remember to write your answer in pencil and in past tense (for example, 'I've been arrogant') in the top triangle of your mandala like the example above.

Emotional Attitudes

Now repeat the exercise, this time noticing your low-self attitude in the area of emotions. Again consider the habit you have already stated for that area and what attitude may sit behind it. Do not judge; simply observe, then record your insight as before ('I've been jealous, resentful, bitter, wounded, fearful, tortured…') in the next triangle round.

Physical Attitudes

Next, identify your attitudes in the physical area. Again, connect with a low-self moment and notice if you were perhaps lethargic, hyperactive, reckless, over-cautious or careless. Can you see a connection with your habit for that area? Write what you believe to be your dominant low-self physical attitude in the next triangle round, worded in pencil and past tense.

Material Attitudes

Now identify your low-self attitudes with regard to wealth and prosperity. Do you see only lack and limitation, causing you to be greedy, grasping, scheming or cocky? Are you flippant, indulgent or wasteful?

Step 2.2

Social Attitudes

The next triangle round represents the social: how do you show up in your relationships when being your low self – passive, aggressive, jealous, closed? Connect with a low-self moment from your past and observe who you were being. Again, record your insight in the past tense (for example, 'I've been judgemental').

Spiritual Attitudes

Finally, what attitudes do you exhibit in the spiritual area of your life when being your low self – is your attitude one of being disconnected, unbelieving, hopeless, unfaithful, indifferent, unworthy? Please remember to state your insight in pencil, and in the past tense. Place it in the last triangle round as per the example.

Step 2.3

Chapter 3

Self-image

Get the Picture

The mental equivalent of a movie, your self-image projects a film of your life to date with you as the star, the cast, the director, editor, audience and critic. The story tells not only of your life-experience and past ways of being, but also of your current outlooks, attitudes and habits.

With your self-image being the main show in town your subconscious is its biggest fan, constantly viewing your internal mental movie in order to keep you the same each and every day. Regularly reinforced or updated by every new thought and experience you have, your self-image is not only the movie for today but also the script for tomorrow.

Follow the Pictures

Like an Ikea picture-instruction manual, your self-image informs you how to *self-assemble*. It supplies you with all the information you need to be you. Whether you see your self as fat or thin, smart or stupid, attractive or ugly, weak or strong, good or bad, likable or not, will all depend on the picture you carry of your *self* inside your head.

When you woke this morning you probably didn't need to invest much time in thinking 'Who am I, and how do I deal with the world?' Chances are you just got up and right on with your day. This is possible because you have a multi-tude of self-image pictures that constantly inform you of *who* you believe you are, *what* you imagine you should do and *how* you should act or react, behave or misbehave in all the varying situations of your day.

Most people will enact dozens of roles and hundreds of scenes in telling their self-image story. There are self-image pictures for what sort of person you think you are *generally*, such as your walk-on roles of sister, brother, parent, partner, friend, col-league, as well as picture-plans for the *specific* repeated activities and learned skills performed within those roles.

For instance, if you drive a car you've probably had this experience: you decide to go somewhere and the next thing you know, you're there. But you can hardly remember the jour-ney: the scenery, actions and manoeuvres you performed along the way.

This common phenomenon, like all other learned skills such as walking or talking, is of course not possible when we are first learning something, because without experience we have little or no detail in our self-image picture for our subconscious to follow. Only gradually, with conscious concentration, do we learn the task at hand. Then, through repetition, we develop our inner mental picture or map. Cause-and-effect feedback from our physical efforts helps us add detail to the map, perfect our ability and our subconscious performance improves.

Athletes know this only too well and will commit much of their training time to visualizing or imagining themselves achieving what they want to achieve. Likewise, some leading emergency service and military training programmes now use visualization to hone trainees' responses and performances.

> Life is the movie you see through your own eyes. It makes little difference what's happening out there. It's how you take it in that counts.
>
> **DENIS WAITLEY**

Picture Perfect

Once the mental picture is established as the *dominant image* for that aspect of our self and life, our subconscious then automatically follows it as the instruction manual for the task at hand. This natural process of our subconscious making us fit the picture of our self-image happens not only with all 'mastered skills' like driving a car, but also as a self-reference for our qualities of character, our ways of being or the *attitude* with which we drive.

Race, nationality, family and affiliations all add to the scenery, the backdrop of our movie. Hear a joke and whether you find it funny or not will depend on whether there is a picture in your self-image of you laughing.

One man's comedy is another's tragedy. We don't all laugh at the same things, have the same experience of life or hold the same beliefs. Your self-image is as individual and unique as your fingerprint. Some of the scenes within it will be of you living from your high Self and being comfortable with your low self, while others will be of you living from your low self and in some form of discomfort, pain or uncertainty. The overall balance of all your images, beliefs and thoughts, high and low, creates your overall sense of self and the general level of comfort or ease you feel within the world.

Mirror, Mirror...

Your self-image is like an inner mirror that reflects a blueprint of who you imagine you are and how you think your life should be. In some ways your self-image acts as your conscience. In a series of experiments scientists placed an open chest of sweets in the middle of an empty room and told children they could go into the room and take one sweet. A hidden camera in the room showed that on most occasions temptation was simply too much and many of the children took a handful of sweets.

However, when a mirror was placed directly behind the chest so that the child could see their reflection they become more self-conscious, and either took only one sweet or, after a few moments of thought, returned the extra sweets. The same dynamic was observed in adults at an office where punctuality for returning from breaks was recorded. Again, when a mirror was introduced to a favourite smoking spot, a marked rise in punctuality was noted.

Highs and Lows

The influence and energies of the high Self and low self sit at the very core of a person's being, causing an effect at every level and layer of self and life. High-Self-image is a picture that is empowered by the qualities of the high Self, such as freedom, clarity and insight, whereas our low-self-image is confined by the traits of our low self: habitual, blinkered and opinionated.

High-Self-image is more than simply positive; the picture is ever developing, ever evolving. The higher your self-image the more transparent your picture will be – like a tranquil lake, it reflects but also allows you to see through. This creates great *response-ability*, enabling you to naturally flow with the moment. The picture we hold of our self is clearer, but also transparent in that it is not fixed. We are open to new insights, as there is always another level of truth to be discovered, our picture is ever changing. In contrast, the low self, being fixed of opinion, is not open to any new insights and therefore the picture, and the person, become stuck.

The lower our self-image falls towards the ego, the more fixed our picture of our self becomes – as if it were etched into the mirror itself, we become rigid and stuck in our ways. The effect is like being limited to just one step on the dance floor of life: regardless of the tune playing, all too often we are wrong-footed.

The Image of Your Self

From infancy on we *reflect on* our experience of life – good or bad, right or wrong, loving or hurtful – and all the while, aware of it or not, we are developing our inner picture and outer image.

A baby will naturally try to copy its parents' smiling faces, and in so doing sends signals to its own brain, releasing serotonin and creating a feeling of happiness. Likewise, other expressions and behaviours in parents cause different chemical releases and create different emotions and behaviour in their children.

Many parents come to realize that children who are smacked learn to smack back. If pushed too hard they push back, and those who are not truly loved do not love back. In the words of William Wordsworth:

> So was it when my life began;
> So is it now I am a man;
> So be it when I shall grow old,
> Or let me die!
> The Child is father of the Man.

Our experience in childhood, what we come to think, feel and believe, shapes our ways of being and the future path into adulthood. Painful experiences early on that are not fully understood and accepted, create blocks in our self-development – they are cracks in our inner mirror that distort our reflection later in life. The deeper the cracks run the more the person's spirit, character and personality become fragmented.

Your Attention Please

The one thing that any child will naturally want more than anything else is your attention. Attention to a child is as important for its mental and emotional development as vitamins are for its physical development.

The earliest image that most babies see, when their eyes begin to focus, is a pair of human eyes gazing lovingly back at them. This connection of direct *unblinking*, *unmasked* eye-contact, parent to child, is repeated often and forms a deep brain-cell connection that is with us for the rest of our lives. We become conditioned to seek comfort and security through eye-contact or attention.

From infancy, a child's high-Self right brain wants to explore. However, the low-self left brain wants to feel safe and secure. While exploring, a young child will constantly be looking to a parent for approval. 'Tell me it's safe', they are saying. 'Give me your attention, play this game with me, talk with me, listen to me, be with me, that I may feel comfort and grow to be confident.'

In contrast, a lack of eye-contact, attention and praise causes varying levels of insecurity. 'I don't feel safe' is the inner thought and feeling, which only results in a greater craving for attention, adoration and respect when older.

Children who are not helped to find comfort in their low self, become adults that forever chase comfort dragons in their life, but never find true comfort. In the competitive chase their ego grows strong and seizes power, but lacking the essential qualities of choice, imagination and empathy, the ego is unequipped to lead and invariably struggles to find the path to true and lasting comfort.

Teenage Turbulence

A child who lacks the stability of connection to their high Self and the authentic confidence that it brings becomes a teenager unsure of their self, easily led down paths that they believe will bring comfort, only to discover that they ultimately lead to pain.

The lower our self-image, the less genuine confidence we have and the more we doubt our self. This imbalance is further disturbed during adolescence, when rapid changes in the body,

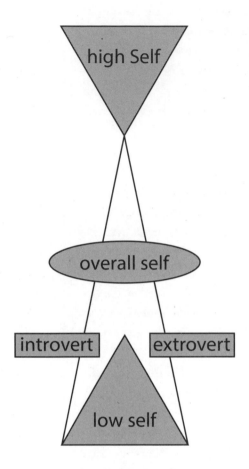

The divided self

mind and emotions can cause a deep sense of uncertainty, often masked by bravado.

Everyone will experience different levels of self-image, in different areas, situations and times of their life. The higher our self-image the greater our inner sense of surety. When our self-image is high our sense of security comes from within us – a strength that we find in our own beliefs and faith in our self. Feeling good about our self, we become open, genuine and live with depth of character.

In contrast, the lower our self-image the less sure of our self we are. We take our sense of security from the outside, from physical possessions and the opinions of others. Most often we try to hide our insecurity either by being shy and introverted, hoping no one will notice us, or by being extroverted and loud, acting outlandishly to cover up the truth.

In either case we are not being our true Self. The deeper we fall into our low-self-image the more we swing from introverted to extroverted, active to reactive, submissive to aggressive in our struggling reactive behaviour.

Sometimes to hide our feelings of discomfort we act extrovertly, showing off and playing the joker. We brag about our abilities or boast of our possessions. At these times our outlooks, attitudes and habits equate to: 'You wish you were like me; I have what you want' or, in essence, 'You want me.'

At other times and in other ways we act shy, introverted and withdrawn. These are the moments when we feel inferior and afraid to show who we really are. In this state our general attitude is most often, 'I wish I was like you; I want what you've got' or 'I want you.'

When we live from our low-self-image we fall into the trap of constantly comparing our self to, and competing with, others. When low, our sense of self comes mainly from whether we believe we measure up against others in terms of looks, abilities or possessions. We feel secure when we do, and insecure when we don't.

> Low-self-image people are totally controlled by winning the good opinion of others.
> ABRAHAM MASLOW

Teenage Turbulence

While our low self-esteem may begin very early in our life, it is in our teenage years, with hormone changes within our body, and social changes within our life, that we really start to feel it, and its effect upon our life. The low self is unsure of itself. It craves a sense of insecurity. When extroverted the low self seeks the attention and validation of others. When introverted it shuns others and seeks the security of seclusion.

Even a balanced child coming into their teenage years with feel the pull of the crowd and the need to be popular. Social media is all about getting 'Likes' from other people. How popular you can be. People with low self-esteem tend not to like themselves or like the way that they are, they are often unsure of themselves and this can result in chasing recognition in the form of 'likes'.

When the self-esteem is low the urge will be to impress by dramatizing everything, to put on a show of bravado and act in all manner of ultimately self-destructive ways, all in a vain attempt to win the good opinion of others or gain attention. The need to be popular, so as to feel sure about their self, drives many teenagers to be someone they are not. They smoke the cigarette they don't enjoy; take the drink they don't want; laugh at the joke they don't find funny; wear the clothes they don't feel comfortable in; mark their and wear the colours of creeds and gangs. All of it is an act to fit in, to feel a connection, to belong in some way, to be comfortable.

There is a growing crises among teenagers with low self-esteem causing mental health challenges, growing levels of self harm, eating disorders and violent behaviour.

The need to be popular has surfaced in the mind of humanity throughout history and across societies. However, in our modern communities, with our interconnected online lives, and masterful manipulation by the media the escalation of low self-esteem in teenagers is rising alarmingly.

A study conducted in England by the Samaritans found teenagers stating that image – trying to live up to the picture painted by other people and the media of how they should look, be and what they should have – was the number-one cause of suicidal thoughts.

Looking Good

As with the child so with the adolescent and likewise the adult; not only do many people never grow out of certain adolescent behaviour, but *humanity* is often adolescent in its outlooks, attitudes and habits.

Our world leaders are too often self-centred; acting from low-self ways of being they steer low-self-driven governments that are focused on manipulation of public opinion and spin, rather than working with genuine quality of character, integrity, openness and public approval, for the common good of all. As with teenagers, politicians feel the need to be popular. We don't really know who our leaders are because when the situation needs direction they are often absent, in person and spirit.

In business, the adolescent low-self qualities of manipulation and greed are too often the drive behind decisions that are largely self-centred, putting profit before people, enrichment at the expense of the environment.

This is also true of many in the media spotlight, such as film stars, pop stars and entertainers. For example, many comedians live from low-self-image: extroverted when onstage and intro-verted when not. In some cases when such people are 'out of character', they don't know who they are, become lost and turn to drink or drugs to find comfort.

And as for so-called reality TV, it is filled with low-self-image sensationalist behaviour in order to grab our attention and head-lines. Perhaps shows like *The Apprentice* would more aptly be renamed *The Egotist*, or *Big Brother* be renamed *Huge Ego*. Most often it is low-self behaviour that surfaces in these programmes as people scramble for the prize.

There is a little low-self-image in all of us, a need to impress others; maybe this is what so fascinates people about these programmes. We would all do well to listen to the advice of William J H Boetcker on this subject:

> That you may retain your self-respect, it is better to displease the people by doing what you know is right, than to temporarily please them by doing what you know is wrong.

The Enchanted Mask

While high-Self-image lives with depth of character, low-self-image displays a thin veneer of personality – a persona or mask. Rarely are we our true Self. Instead we put on an act, hoping it will impress so we can fit in at the office, the school gate, and even in our own home, but this behaviour usually results in us feeling uncomfortable, stiff and awkward.

In some people, just as in some societies, the veneer, the act, is very thin, but the mask still blocks them from seeing the truth in their self and life. It is as if they have forgotten they're

> For beautiful eyes,
> look for the good in others;
> for beautiful lips,
> speak only words of kindness;
> and for poise, walk with the knowledge that you are never alone.
>
> **AUDREY HEPBURN**

wearing a mask; they look through the eyeholes and see a reflection of their own outlook, mirrored back to them through their experience of life. Those who look for bitterness find bitterness. Those who seek joy discover bliss.

If you are blind to the truth about your self, then you will also be blind to the truth in others, and ignorant to the truth of life.

Funny Mirrors

My own childhood was an interesting mix of homes and life-experience. My family travelled around the country operating funfair equipment and setting up entertainments. Our summers were usually spent at Ventnor on the Isle of Wight where my father ran an amusement arcade on the pier. One of the attractions was a hall of mirrors. The mirrors were not straight, but rather concave and convex. Each one reflected a slightly warped version of you – some reflections were fat, others thin; some short, others tall.

Most people have the equivalent of a hall of mirrors inside their head. The reflection they see is not their true Self, but a slightly warped picture of their self, which causes distorted attitudes and twisted behaviours.

In some people the twisted mirror becomes dominant and causes a much more distorted self-image. Illnesses and eating disorders such as anorexia nervosa usually start in bright teenagers with low self-image. They develop a 'funny mirror', a distorted picture of their self that clouds their perception. When they look in a real mirror they don't see what is really there; they see a distortion and imagine they are fat, when in reality they are painfully thin.

People whose low self is dominant are overly concerned about how they appear to others. It's all about their image. They constantly compare themselves to other people, feeling good when they have more, and worse when they have less.

In contrast, people whose high Self is stronger see beyond the reflection to the truth of their Self, others and reality. The higher the self-image the more solid they become, showing openly who they are, and seeing their Self clearly. They draw their security from the inside, from *who they are as a person*, knowing that life can only be lived fully if it is lived with Spirit from the true Self. They understand that the true quest of life is to be *their* best, not *the* best.

> **Our very business in life is not to get ahead of others... but to get ahead of ourselves.**
> THOMAS MONSON

Life's a Mirror

The Bible tells us that we are each created in the image of the Creator. Not, of course, that we look like God, but that we each carry a reflection of the divine in our high Self. We are each the creators of our own realities. Whether consciously or unconsciously, in harmony or discord, who we are being in our *self*, high or low, is reflected in the quality of what we create in our *life*. People with a good self-image (whose high Self is strong) create a little bit of heaven regardless of their situation or circumstance while people with a low self-image are forever making their life hell.

The Third Commandment of the Old Testament reads: 'Do not worship graven images.' I see this as saying 'do not follow the false image of your low self', for it too is an engraved image, a fixed picture of your self. When our self-image is unbalanced it releases the beast in man and we act the very devil, in our work, our relationships and even with our own families.

Predominantly low-self-image people see a distorted picture of life and tend to be ego-centred, slipping easily into the rut of blaming, bullying, justifying or conforming. They are anything other than their true Self, and instead are constantly putting on a front, a mask or persona.

The need to be popular, or feel superior, often results in friction and trouble. People with low-self-image believe that they've got to be 'the best', better than everyone else, rather than simply seeking to be *their* best. They need to be right about everything, win all the arguments and always have the last word. Of course they have many justifications for this, as they have grown up hearing it from their own parents as the 'right' way to be.

If they make a decision that isn't working they are slow to change it because they see any form of mistake as a real weakness. If someone else does something well they are slow to praise, and they are quick to punish when things go wrong. When life shows them that they are off track, seldom do they take true responsibility and instead point the finger of blame. They are opinionated, manipulative and vindictive. And most often they are completely blind to all of it, instead finding fault in others for the very things they are oblivious of in their self.

People Are Mirrors

People unconsciously look for a mirror image of their self in others, seeking a measure of beauty, fitness or interest that reflects their own. Studies indicate that facial resemblance between couples is much higher than would be expected from random pairing.

Generally we are attracted to people we imagine to be like us; they reflect an image that is familiar and therefore we feel comfortable with them. In contrast, the people we find to be very different from us, in opinions, attitudes, actions and looks, are not normally people we feel much connection with. They may be interesting but they are *unfamiliar* and therefore we are less comfortable in their presence.

Often we are attracted to someone, or someone is attracted to us, because they have or we have something the other is looking for, such as confidence. Self-belief and surety are attractive in a person, while desperation and insecurity are repulsive. Regardless of how the person looks, even

> A loving person lives in a loving world. A hostile person lives in a hostile world. Everyone you meet is your mirror.
> **KEN KEYES**

if physically attractive, if they give off the wrong vibe we inevitably leave. Only when both people find a reflection of their self in their partner does the relationship stick.

The world is full of broken marriages with incomplete people looking to their partner to compensate for their own shortcomings. In truth, it takes two whole people to make one good marriage.

Seeing Your Low Self

Before you can move on to the *ideal* you must be clear about the *actual* – the current before the desired. You must be conscious of who you are, your low-self egotistical behaviours, before you can become your true Self.

This is easier said than done, as once the low-self ego is dominant it clings to power and fights against anything that will dissolve it, especially information about itself. It's like an undercover agent: it doesn't want to be detected, let alone studied. It lies, tricks, threatens and manipulates, all to stay in control.

If, right now, you are saying, 'I have no ego', you can be sure that is your *ego* doing the talking.

One way to spot your ego is to look at what really annoys you. For instance, if your outlook is: 'nobody believes in me', chances are the insight to be gained is: 'I don't believe in my self.' Outlook: 'nobody loves me'; insight: 'I don't love my self.' Outlook: 'nobody listens to me'; insight: 'I don't listen.'

> Everything that irritates us about others can lead us to an understanding of ourselves.
> CARL JUNG

What's Your Comfort Blankey?

Another way of seeing your self is through your behaviours and habits. What are you addicted to?

From the moment she was born I watched in complete awe as my baby daughter showed signs of craving the comfort she had known before her birth. She came to rely on certain things for comfort: first the tight-wrapped swaddling, then the breast, the bottle, the thumb, and now at four and half it's the 'blankey'.

We all find 'comfort blankets', as we attach feelings of pleasure to external stimulants. This invariably leads the majority of people to spend their entire lives *looking for* and *clinging to* comfort blankets of all description. Sometimes we think we've outgrown these things but the need for them resurfaces during times of stress, when we take that drink, smoke that fag, indulge our lust, all to ease our discomfort.

What's your 'comfort blanket'? Think about your self, particularly those behaviours that you don't like to acknowledge, and ask your self: are they acts of your high-Self spirit, or habits of your low-self ego?

— ◆ —

IN ESSENCE

The essence to remember and live from in this chapter is:

Cultivate a mental image
of being your true Self.

Creating Your Self Map

Freeing questions to ask your self for this chapter are:

◆ Does being with different groups of people cause you to *be different* in your self?

◆ Are you overly concerned about your appearance and the impression you make when attending regular events such as collecting the kids from school or shopping?

◆ Do you feel the need to let others know about your achievements?

Step 3 – Low-self Outlooks

By this stage you may be noticing that some of the same low-self qualities or ways of being are coming up more than once for various areas of your life. This is quite normal and simply indicates that this is a dominant way of being for you. You will find it rewarding to dig deeper and look for the quality that sits behind it.

Once again if you have any gaps or are unsure, simply continue with the next step and trust that the insight will come to you as you explore your self further. Likewise you can change or add any new insights to your existing statements before continuing.

Mental Outlook

The final part of filling in your low-self mandala involves identifying your outlooks. Once again, connect with a low-self moment and notice your dominant mental outlook or viewpoint. For example, when low do you see your self as inferior or superior? What is your main opinion or belief about your self? Do you believe you are stupid or useless?

As before, think about what you have already stated as your habit and attitude for this area and consider what outlook may sit behind them. You will often find your outlooks reflected in the things you say to your self at low times, such as 'I'm so stupid; I always get it wrong!' Then write down your outlook, in pencil and the past tense, in the top inner triangle of your mandala.

Emotional Outlook

When being your low self, what's your dominant outlook or picture of your self? Are you, for instance, fearful, sad, depressed or hateful?

Step 3.1

Look again at your previous statements in this area and check for connections or reflections. If your habit is 'I have acted aggressively' and is reflected in the attitude of 'I have been angry', then maybe the belief or outlook that drives them is 'I have felt self-hatred.' Remember to record your insight in pencil and past tense, placed in the next inner triangle.

Physical Outlook

What picture or outlook do you hold of your physical self in a low-self moment? Are you disgusted with or ashamed of your body? Do you see your self as being dirty, damaged or incomplete? Again, write your insight in the past tense.

Material Outlook

What is your low-self outlook with regard to the material aspects of your life? Do you see money as evil, scarce or dirty?

Step 3.2

Is your outlook one of lack and limitation? When low, do you believe you are the victim of circumstance?

Social Outlook

The next triangle is the social. What's your low-self outlook with regard to your relationships? Are you shy or showy? Are you intolerant, indifferent, dependent, resentful or smug?

Spiritual Outlook

The last triangle of the mandala represents the spiritual. Connect with a low-self moment and observe without judgement your outlooks with regard to your self and a sense of purpose. Do you see your self as sinful, doubting, lost, isolated, meaningless, alone or disconnected?

Write your final statement as before in pencil and the past tense. Look at the freeing questions to overcome blocks and complete any remaining spaces.

Step 3.3

Part Two

Feeling

Chapter 4

Self-esteem

It cannot be bought at any price, yet people think that wealth will bring it. Neither does it necessarily come with title or talent, for there are many high-born and famous people who wish to possess it. The most pepping of tonics, the most effective of cosmetics and the best booster of power, it is sought by everyone. And although it is absolutely free, few are prepared to pay the true price to attain it. Those that have it have everything. Those without it may sometimes seem to have everything, but in truth have nothing.

An Ocean of Emotion

Imagine that every emotion you've ever felt has never really left you and instead adds to an inner sea of self-esteem. An ocean of emotion, regularly rising and falling, where angry emotions stir up stormy seas, unexpressed emotions stagnate into dead seas and loving emotions create peaceful, calm seas.

While we will all experience fair winds and choppy waters within the seasons and cycles of our life, it is the overall balance of all our emotions that together create the tidemark of our self-esteem – the measure of how much we like our self.

In Your Estimation

The word 'esteem' stems from the Latin *aestimo*, 'to value or esti-mate'. Your 'self-esteem' is *your estimation of your self*. It is how much you value your self, your sense of self-worth.

While people and situations can have an influence on your self-esteem, at essence, it's *your* estimation of *your self* that results in *your esteem* regardless of the opinions others may hold.

A recent finalist of a national talent contest was asked what it would mean to him if he won. He answered almost instantly that he had low self-esteem and winning would finally allow him to feel good about himself. In reality it is not the thing or achievement that creates or destroys our self-esteem but our estimation of it. One person may achieve something really wonderful but not be pleased with their self, while another will do something seemingly simple but take great satisfaction from their accomplishment.

There are countless people who can do extraordinarily talent-ed things, appearing to live seemingly wonderful lives, and often accumulating tremendous wealth and accolades, yet they feel poor in their self-esteem and unhappy with their life.

Princess Diana, Marilyn Monroe and Elvis Presley are classic examples of how public adulation will not automatically bring true self-esteem. Many celebrities, entertainers, sports stars and politicians seem to glow with assurance when 'performing', but offstage in their private lives they may be unsure of their self and feel desperately insecure.

> No one can make you feel inferior without your consent.
> **ELEANOR ROOSEVELT**

In truth, nobody and nothing can give you self-esteem. It is a do-it-yourself task to learn to like your self. Likewise, nobody can really take self-esteem away from you either, unless you decide to let go of it.

Right now, without comparing your self to another, where would you place your feelings of esteem about your self, high or low, to the following:

high

low

◆ Are you honestly comfortable with your self and happy in your outlooks?

◆ Do you feel you're a good person, have the right attitudes and genuinely deserve good fortune, love and success?

◆ Are you comfortable with your habits and the circumstances you've attracted or created in your life?

Highs and Lows – Inner and Outer

Our answers to such questions often depend on whether we feel up or down, or are having a good or bad day. However, while we will all experience periods of high and low self-esteem in response to the ebb and flow of life's tides, it is the people with generally high self-esteem that find it much easier to answer 'yes' to the above, not because of their achievements, but because at essence they are *comfortable* with their self. They live their life more fully from their high Self and through it feel a deep inner security that they are OK as a person, whatever their level of accomplishment.

However, when our self-estimation is driven by the energies of our low self, our ego grasps at 'straws of security' which are invariably taken from the outside: in how we look, what we can do or the possessions we have in comparison to others.

When our esteem comes from our high Self our sense of worth is drawn from within and centres on an estimation of whether we are in harmony with the qualities of our Self, such as living with spirit, being true to our beliefs or values and guided by a sense of faith or purpose.

> It is not the man who has too little, but the man who craves more, that is poor.
> **SENECA**

Am I OK?

Years ago I had a friend who felt the need to constantly try to impress everyone. While at heart a good person, his insecurity caused him to act in strange ways. He often played the know-all, the bragger. Whatever anyone else may have done, seen or achieved, he had already done it, knew all about it and had the T-shirt to prove it.

We all know someone like this. Typically such people will only wear what they believe will impress others, the clothes that have the right labels. They need all the latest gadgets, not normally to use, but to show off with. They drive the flashiest car, usually one they can't really afford, live way beyond their means and talk loudly about their achievements at every opportunity.

Their bravado is often mistaken for confidence. In truth, they are desperately insecure. Behind the mask, at a subconscious level, they are saying, 'Please be impressed with me and all these things I know, can do, or have. Because deep down I'm not impressed with my self, I'm unsure of my self and I need your approval to tell me I'm OK.'

> What I am is good enough if I would only be it openly.
> **CARL ROGERS**

Virtually everyone knows someone like this because, while it may be uncomfortable to acknowledge, virtually everyone has some element of this within their self. We will all at times feel vulnerable, suffer low self-esteem and put on an act to hide our insecurity and try to prove our worth.

Look at My Things

I first noticed my low self-esteem, and the accompanying need to impress others, when I was 19. I was on holiday in a beautiful tropical resort with ten of my friends, but I started thinking, 'I wish I had my car here to cruise in. I wish I had my disco here to entertain in. I wish I had my...' Then I suddenly thought, 'Why do I want those things here? I'm on holiday having a great time.'

And a little voice whispered in my head, 'Because those things are your security and without them you're *nothing*.'

I found the realization that I was insecure so shocking that I shut the door on it in my head and heart, refusing to acknowledge the insight. Some 11 years later, around age 30, I was forced to confront the truth: my business sank into insolvency, my wife left, my belongings were repossessed, and with them my false sense of confidence, stemming from what I owned or controlled, crashed.

Often when I am sharing my story in my workshops, someone else will have the same profound realization: that their confidence is really bravado and that they actually have low self-esteem. In one particular seminar a young man, who had bragged loudly all morning about his achievements, realized that people could see through his mask. Feeling insecure, he went on the attack: 'So you're saying it's not right to have nice things, are you then; that we should all live in poverty?'

> It is the heart that makes a man rich. He is rich according to what he is, not according to what he has.
>
> HENRY WARD BEECHER

'Not at all', I answered. 'Experience them. Use them. Enjoy them. The question is: why do you want them?'

Do you want your things because you genuinely believe they will improve your quality of life, or do you need them to feel secure? If it is the latter, no number of possessions will ever fill the hole inside you and you will always experience poverty in your self.

Life only truly becomes fulfilling when lived with spirit from our high Self, taking our sense of worth from the inside.

Self-starter

Of course no one is born with either low or high self-esteem; it is something we develop. My baby daughter Ayesha doesn't look in the mirror and think to herself, 'This bib gives me a double chin and that makes me feel sad, although I've got great legs for a nappy, so I feel good.' Her self-esteem, like that of all other children, begins by attaching feelings to experiences and gradually the inner ocean of emotion starts to fill.

While ultimately it is our estimation of our self that results in our level of self-esteem, many things can influence our opinion, particularly when we are young, and lead us into a low evaluation of our self. Some people develop low self-esteem through lack of encouragement, being overly criticized or shouted at. Sometimes experiences at school or work cause us to feel weak or stupid. Moving away from friends to a new area can lower self-esteem, as can being bullied or feeling abandoned by loved ones.

The Comparison Trap

One of the most common causes of low self-esteem starts at a very early age when we are not even fully conscious that it is happening; the excessive comparison to others or being excessively measured against external criteria for someone's opinion of what is success. If a young child is heavily pushed to achieve, if they are overly compared to others (such as, 'Why can't you be more like your brother or sister? The other children seem to manage fine'). If the love from the parent is lacking or conditional, the child will subconsciously conclude: 'I am not loved just for being me. I am only loved when I'm as good as them, which must mean that they are better than me and I am less than them, I must do better.' Gradually we form the limiting and false belief that: 'I'm not good enough.'

Over time, the constant comparison fuels the feeling that we are 'worth less' than other people. Gradually the feeling grows into a deep sense of 'worthlessness' that we are not of value, not as good as others. As we grow the feeling deepens, although we are most often unaware of its cause, and we become increasingly conditioned to constantly compare our self to others measuring our worth in terms of how well we live up to the people around us and our society's ever-changing opinions of what makes a 'successful person'. In adult life our benchmarks of success become increasingly external; the university we attended, the qualifications we achieved, the work we do and our position in it, the home that we live it, the car that we drive, the holiday we take. And regardless of what we may achieve, always in the shadow of our mind and heart will be the thought and feeling that we not really good enough, lowering our self-esteem and affecting through our behaviour every area and aspect of our life.

To escape the trap, we must learn to re-condition our self to only compare our progress in our journey back home to our True Self. Are we continuing our path with another step towards living our life from our True Self beliefs, attitudes and behaviours? Are we living with integrity, in accordance with our highest values? Are we following life's Golden Rule of treating others the way you would wish to be treated? These are the criteria by which to measure our progress of what is most important in life. It is an inner journey of success leading to ever-greater levels of happiness and peace regardless of our outer material success or other people's opinion of it.

Scar Tissue of the Mind

As you make your way in the world it is inevitable that you will stumble and fall many times. Fortunately, people have a wonderful ability to heal. Cut yourself and your body responds by mending the wound and growing some new skin. What's more, your deeper awareness recognizes that the area may have been weak and replaces the damage with slightly thicker, tougher scar tissue.

In like manner, we will all *mentally* and *emotionally* fall many times, feel all cut up inside, and again form scar tissue, only this time to protect the mind and emotions. Each time we become torn in heart or head by some painful experience, lack of love or unjust comparison, which we do not come to terms with, we form mental and emotional scar tissue that hardens our attitudes, stiffens our behaviour and scales over our eyes. This is the formation of ego – the mask we wear to protect ourselves. The lower our self-esteem falls, the more uncomfortable we feel with our self, and the thicker our mask of ego becomes.

The Birth of Ego

The ego is our sense of low self born out of our experience of life and the realization that we are separate from it. Being of the low self, our ego possesses low-level consciousness and is mainly concerned with awareness of the physical body, time and the material world. The ego's two main roles are those of protector and provider, and thus by its very nature it is self-centred and self-serving. That's not to say the ego isn't wonderful, for it's truly a spark of the divine – an individual wave in the ocean of consciousness travelling free on its path.

> A difficult time can be more readily endured if we retain the conviction that our existence holds a purpose – a cause to pursue, a person to love, a goal to achieve.
> **JOHN MAXWELL**

There was a magical moment when my daughter progressed from saying 'Shanti did it' or 'It's Shanti's' to 'I did it' and 'It's mine.' This critical-mass point of consciousness reached by all children through the connection of brain cells and formation of beliefs is the birth of ego. It's the vital first step in becoming our self, an individual person, self-sufficient, self-reliant and self-determining.

Individualization is a painful process. The descent from 'we' of collective consciousness and birth of 'I' involves struggle and effort. Like a butterfly breaking free from its cocoon we must each reach for life. We are empowered in our effort by the natural drive of evolution. The life-pulse fuels the ego, which needs no encouragement to compete, naturally wanting to be the best of the species, the prettiest, cleverest, strongest and fastest. This is the primeval urge to grow, survive and thrive. At first, like a surge from a newly tapped wellspring, the ego comes gushing out to swamp all other qualities and personal energies.

Observe the self-centredness of even the most cared-for and balanced child as their ego emerges and they become a tyrant totally absorbed in *their self*, *their needs* and having it all *their way*. If the child isn't helped back into balance by connecting with their high Self they become trapped in low self-esteem and live from the ego's unbalanced characteristics; sometimes being nervous, lethargic and submissive, and other times impatient, intolerant, demanding and stubborn.

The Turning Point of Purpose

Children and adults thrive on learning new things; it's a drive encoded in our genes and helps us keep growing in our self. At any age, setting and achieving even the simplest of goals can lift our self-esteem, help us feel good about our self and move us forward in life.

> Your purpose explains what you are doing with your life. Your vision explains how you are living your purpose. Your goals enable you to realize your vision.
>
> **BOB PROCTOR**

There are many forms of goal, vision or purpose that empower people, and all are connected like pearls on a string.

The prime goals or drives of the low self are to secure food, shelter and clothing – the sustenance of life; while the pull of our high Self is to find meaning, order and purpose in the chaos of existence. The high Self seeks to consciously understand what it intuitively knows: that there is a reason for living, that we are here for a purpose and that reality extends beyond the physical.

People have always felt the call of their high Self over the din of their low self, the urge to seek the truth and find their place in the world. And while there are many paths in life that can be taken, vocations, achievements and worthy causes to pursue, everyone's prime purpose, their inner purpose, is simply to be their best.

By seeking to be *our* best, rather than competing against others to be *the* best, we turn a corner in our development and begin the journey back home to source, reuniting with our high Self, to become our true Self. It is everyone's personal prime directive; a spiritual imperative. It is what Muhammad called 'the greater jihad' – the struggle to improve your self and, through it, find your Self.

All great teachers have shared this same truth. Jesus said:

> Let him who seeks not cease from seeking
> until he finds;

and when he finds,
he will be turned around;
and when he is turned around he will marvel,
and he shall reign over the All.

GOSPEL OF THOMAS

Seek the path within your self by asking soul-searching questions: Why am I here? What's life all about? How do I fit into it? When we focus within our self for our answers, question our beliefs, examine our behaviour and listen to the whisper of intuition, we find the path to our true Self. We are *turned around* or transformed in the process. We marvel at the beauty of creation that now unfolds before our eyes. And having found the power of the Kingdom within, we act with integrity from the positive energies of our high Self and everything else in the Kingdom is added to us.

Be first, before you *do*, and then you will *have*. By leading your life from your high Self with the energies of love and compassion, while managing from your head with consideration and strategy, you find your intuitive response and naturally flow towards your chosen desires.

People who live from their low self want to *have* first, often without *doing*, and rarely question their ways of *being*. They become reactive, driven by fear to chase food, shelter and clothing. As no amount of these things can ever really bring true comfort, they never move on to find genuine meaning and purpose or contentment in their self and life.

In contrast, when you pursue the inner path towards your true Self, you find meaning and purpose *first*; then through it you attract food, shelter and clothing in abundance. In this way, you can fulfil your secondary purpose: finding the things you choose to *do* and *have*. Empowered by your *being*, you can live harmoniously with power and satisfaction.

> First say to yourself what you would be; and then do what you have to do.
> EPICTETUS

Self-certification

Setting standards and values for your self and holding to them is the path to high-Self-esteem. The more you harmoniously align your behaviours and goals with your own standards and values, the more you will grow to respect your self and the higher your self-esteem will rise.

Do something with your life that you regard as worthwhile and your self-esteem will soar. One of the keys is to use your time wisely, as this extract from Al Ghazzali's *The Alchemy of Happiness* explains:

> At the resurrection a man will find all the hours of his life arranged like a long series of treasure-chests. The door of one will be opened, and it will be seen to be full of light: it represents an hour which he spent in doing good. His heart will be filled which such joy that even a fraction of it would make the inhabitants of hell forget the fire. The door of a second will be opened; it is pitch-dark within, and from it issues such an evil odour as will cause everyone to hold his nose: it represents an hour which he spent in ill-doing, and he will suffer such terror that a fraction of it would embitter Paradise for the blessed. The door of a third treasure-chest will be opened; it will be seen to be empty and neither light nor dark within: this represents the hour in which he did neither good nor evil. Then he will feel remorse and confusion like that of a man who has been the possessor of a great treasure and wasted it or let it slip from his grasp. Thus the whole series of the hours of his life will be displayed, one by one, to his gaze. Therefore a man should say to his soul every morning, 'God has given thee 24 treasures; take heed lest thou lose any one of them, for thou wilt not be able to endure the regret that will follow such loss.'

Heart Song

The key to honouring your life and creating true self-esteem is to learn to like your self, just the way that you are. Learn to like your weight, shape, possessions and life; be genuinely grateful.

True gratitude is joyous, not mournful.

Do not fall into the trap of doing what other people think you 'should do' how you 'should look' what you 'should have'. Do not buy into stereotypes without due consideration. If you are setting goals based on what you think you should do rather than on what you truly desire to do, it is very likely that you are going to actually lower your self-esteem.

Instead – to support your inner purpose of becoming your true Self; living with Spirit and anchoring a little more of heaven here on earth – seek an outer purpose that helps you to be truly joyous. Life was never meant to be drudgery.

Find that thing that makes your heart sing. Find a sense of purpose that you feel truly passionate about. Something that is bigger than your low self, grander than your ego, larger than your existing comfort zone, something that will cause you to stretch and grow your self-esteem.

> To a happy person, the formula for happiness is quite simple: Regardless of what [has] happened ... or what may happen ... now is where happiness lies.
>
> RICHARD CARLSON

Follow your prime purpose first and foremost, and as you develop, so you will grow your sense of self-worth, which will in turn help you to clarify and pursue your outer purpose, dreams and goals.

Wherever you are right now, and whatever you are doing, your purpose is waiting for you. Do not wait to find the outer thing before travelling the inner path, as through its illumination you will be shown your way.

Not so many years ago most people were told their purpose in life by the church, the lord of the manor, the place in society they were born into or their family. Now, more people are freer than ever before to choose their own way. But that freedom comes with a price: you must seek out and pursue a personal sense of meaning and purpose – a reason for being.

Your outer purpose can be whatever you choose: your family, your faith, your society, your work, your hobby or sport.

While our inner purpose is always an individual path, the outer purpose can be a collective endeavour. A united sense of purpose has birthed nations, created enduring monuments, forged world-changing movements, united communities and raised great families. When hearts and minds join, power is increased and untold wonders are achieved, the effects of which positively affect the lives of many.

The Hundredth Monkey Theory

In 1952 a team of scientists travelled to the isolated Pacific island of Koshima to study a colony of macaque monkeys. To entice them into view, sweet potatoes were laid on the ground. One day a young female monkey discovered that washing the mud off the potatoes made them taste better and promptly taught this new insight to her sister. Together they taught others, who taught still more monkeys. When a critical-mass point was reached, of around 100 monkeys, suddenly all the monkeys on the island, and others from the mainland, started washing their potatoes without being physically taught the trick.

While the science is not fully proven the concept of 'the hundredth monkey' – that we are all connected to a collective consciousness which can shift when a critical-mass point is reached – has examples throughout history. People separated by great distances, without means of communication, have come up with the same ideas at the same time; cultures have developed along parallel paths, and the same great truths have been realized.

> Until you value yourself you will not value your time. Until you value your time, you will not do anything with it.
>
> **MORGAN SCOTT PECK**

> Your Purpose is what you say it is; your Mission is the mission you give yourself; your life will be what you create it as and no one will stand in judgement of it now or ever.
>
> **NEALE DONALD WALSH**

Many studies show that when enough people raise their awareness and become their true Self, their energy has an effect on others around them in the area. In 1993 a group of 4,000 volunteers gathered in Washington to evaluate the effects of united positive focus on the city. During the days of their meditation a 25 per cent drop in violent crime was recorded.

Collective consciousness is truly universal. It knows no bounds. All is one, and a single one can trigger the tipping point affecting the All.

We can each make a difference, and a key question to ask your self is: What if you are the hundredth monkey? What if evolving your self to become your true Self is the final tipping-point that helps trigger a higher level of consciousness which positively affects others in your family, your community or humanity?

Shakespeare knew it and expressed it thus:

> There is a tide in the affairs of men,
> Which, taken at the flood, leads on to fortune;
> Omitted, all the voyage of their life
> Is bound in shallows and in miseries.

JULIUS CAESAR **IV, III, 217**

— ◆ —

IN ESSENCE

The essence to remember and live from in this chapter is:

*Learn to like your low self
and your true Self
will blossom.*

Creating Your Self Map

Ask your self these freeing questions:

◆ What purpose has your life already served?

◆ What makes your heart sing?

◆ How much do you like your self?

Step 4 – High-Self Habits

Breathe Easy

Sit with your back upright, your hands palm-up on your knees. Let the thumb and first finger of each hand meet to form a loop. Take three deep breaths, in through your nose and out through your mouth, saying 'relax' on each out-breath.

Do it *now*!

Now, curl your other fingers round into a loop, fingertips pointing towards the palms (so as to form two tubes), and take three more deep breaths, in through your nose and out through your mouth, this time repeating 'I am' on each out-breath.

Finally, lay your thumbs across your palms and close your fingers around them, take three more deep breaths as before, close your eyes, move beyond any story of who you think you are, *be still* and know you are a child of the universe, no more or less than the stars.

Mental Habits

Connect with your high Self, by focusing on a magical moment from your past, a moment when you have flowed from your Self. Who were you being in that moment?

Now imagine pursuing your purpose, living your dreams and achieving your goals. Who will you need to be in order

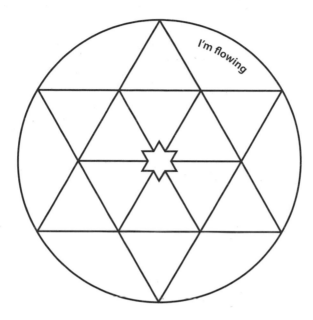

I'm flowing

Step 4.1

to achieve them? Which qualities of character, outlooks, attitudes, behaviours and habits will most empower your high Self and thereby everything you do and have in your life?

Be that way now and notice your main habit mentally. Are you patient, poised, focused, responsible and determined?

Remember, this is an intuitive exercise. Trust your first thoughts, then write your statement in a new Self Mapping mandala, this time using a **pen for permanence** and worded in the **present tense** in the top-right outer triangle of your mandala as in the example above.

Emotional Habits

Flow on through, staying connected to your high Self, either by remembering a past moment or choosing to be your Self now, and notice your main way of behaving *emotionally*. Are you, for instance, cheerful, witty, assertive, passionate or brave?

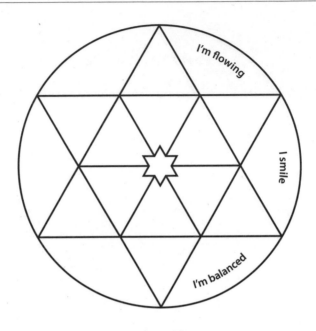

Step 4.2

Go with what feels right, or if you are stuck look for the positive opposite of your low-self statement. For example, if your low-self statement is 'I haven't been caring' then maybe your positive opposite is 'I care.'

Physical Habits

Next consider your physical habits. Stay connected to your high Self and observe how you behave in this area. Are you vibrant, energetic, relaxed, calm, active or flexible?

As before, trust your intuition and write your statement in pen and present tense in the relevant outer triangle.

Material Habits

Now take note of your material habits and actions when living from your high Self. Are you considerate, generous, giving,

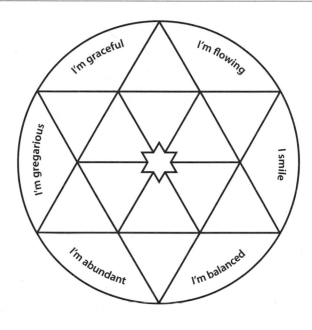

Step 4.3

fair and charitable? Once again, write your statement in pen and in the present tense.

Social Habits

Next, observe how you are acting with regard to relationships. When being your high Self are you respectful, courteous, honest, praising, kind and committed? Remember, trust your intuition, then state your insight in the next triangle round.

Spiritual Habits

Finally, to complete the outer circle, notice how you are acting or behaving with regard to a sense of spirit, meaning and purpose. When being your high Self are you graceful, peaceful, elegant, natural and authentic? Then write in the last outer circle as per the example.

Chapter 5

Self-acceptance

Do What Thou Wilt, Shall Be the Whole of the Law.

So wrote Aleister Crowley, expressing the ancient view that each person's sole responsibility is to accept the will of their high Self, which knows the true path, rather than the whim of their low self, which is driven by the ego.

> I would not waste my life in friction when it could be turned into momentum.
> **FRANCES WILLARD**

Following the will of our high Self, the path of prime purpose, is not the easy 'do as you damn well please' option it may first appear. On the contrary, it's a journey that will of necessity lead us away from any low-self false comfort zones and addictions, even to suffer the pangs of craving and face confrontation, in order to ultimately reach the eternal, deeply satisfying complete comfort of our true Self. It is a journey that will invariably require growing levels of acceptance with our high and low selves, situation and society, for each step of progress that we make.

Highs and Lows

Humans are social creatures; one of our most basic needs is to be accepted by an individual or a group. While our high Self, our spiritual self, is completely accepting, our low self is fear-driven and seeks to protect and reject and, in turn, it also fears rejection.

Scientists conducted a game where three people threw a ball back and forth. One of the participants was unaware that the other two were part of the experiment. These two followed a pre-arranged plan of only throwing the ball to each other. Just a few moments of being excluded were enough for most people to show feelings of sadness and anger. The same happened even with an electronic version of the game called Cyberball. It would seem that people can even feel rejected by a computer.

The lower our self-image, self-esteem, self-worth, etc., the more suspicious and fearful of others we are. At the same time we still crave acceptance, to the point where we surrender our own values and do things that are not for the highest good. All too often our desire for acceptance results in some form of partial defeat or negative compromise of our aims and ambitions.

In contrast, it is genuinely sublime to live in a true state of acceptance; it is a victory gained through an awareness of our low self, our high Self, human nature and the workings of life's laws.

Living in a state of true acceptance means living with awareness that everything happens for a reason and a purpose; that we can learn from everything, the good as well as the bad, the desired as well as the undesired, and ultimately benefit from everything, if we choose to accept it.

Accept your plight and make light of it. Accept *what*, *where* and *who* you are right now. Accept all of you. Your high Self *and* low self; accept all of your attitudes and habits, including those you really don't like. Accept society, especially anyone you don't currently see eye-to-eye with, those that appear *wrong* in your eyes. And practise acceptance with the situations and circumstance of your life, the things that irritate or stress you.

> Accept everything about yourself – I mean everything. You are you and that is the beginning and the end – no apologies, no regrets.
> **CLARK MOUSTAKAS**

Bend Like the Willow

Your acceptance of things or aspects of your self doesn't mean you agree with them or won't change them in the future. It simply means that you stop thrashing against them now, in the present, and instead gracefully flow beyond by focusing on what's next.

The way of acceptance from the true Self is to bend like the willow; it is *movement with repose*. Like a meandering river, its purpose is to flow. It knows its ultimate goal, which is reunion with the sea. It accepts its natural surroundings, while still pursuing its general course. With twists and turns it rushes and falls, floods and narrows. And although the river always accepts the path of least resistance, even the hardest of rocks and deepest of ravines do not deter it. Indeed, the greatest of obstacles are invariably changed by it, as it rolls relentlessly on towards a reunion with the ocean.

Accept a Little Harmony in Your Life

We are each like a great river, and by practising acceptance from the true Self, we create harmony in the flow of our life. Being able to accept things is like swimming with the current; we progress more easily and faster towards our ultimate destination. True-Self acceptance is directly wedded to self-esteem; the greater our level of acceptance, the higher our esteem will lift in reunion with our true Self.

In contrast, low-self resistance and fighting against aspects of our self or circumstance produce blocks in our emotions, such as suppressed anger, which become like rocks lying in the bed of the river. When the flow is slow they go mostly unnoticed. But when the pace quickens and we begin to feel the stress, pressure and rush of life, then like in a river, the blocks cause great turbulence in the flow and we end up fighting against the current.

We may achieve what we want but it comes slowly and at great cost. Much of our energy is drained in the struggle, and by egotistically forcing our way against the natural flow, we often bring about something that's not for our highest good.

Accept Response-ability

Our greatest gift is our free will. We are each, at the deepest level, free to choose our thoughts and thereby our feelings. It is one of the hallmarks of true humanity that our response to situations, our outlooks, our attitudes, our actions, our ways of being, are not set in stone, not fixed by our genes – they are choices that we can make in each and every moment, regardless of circumstance.

Exercise the will of your high Self now, by choosing to accept *who* you are, *where* you are and *what* you have, and in so doing you will free your self to move on and become who you choose to be.

Creating harmony in your life starts by accepting the *whole* you, so that you start swimming in the same direction. You can begin accepting it now, simply by choosing the quality of your thoughts about your self. Try it, just for a moment; tell your self that it's all OK. Let go of any resistance, regret or reservation. Ease your mind and be at peace with your self.

How Does It Feel?

When we practise choosing acceptance, with our self, life and society, regardless of our situation, we nourish our self and come into bloom.

Choosing acceptance is not a one-off choice, but one of many that are made in the stream of our life. All choices are made in the moment, and from moment to moment. Acceptance therefore, like response-ability, is an ongoing journey of choices.

> Love the moment. Flowers grow out of dark moments. Therefore, each moment is vital. It affects the whole. Life is a succession of such moments and to live each, is to succeed.
>
> **CORITA KENT**

> In the long run, we shape our lives, and we shape ourselves. The process never ends until we die. And the choices we make are ultimately our own responsibility.
>
> **ELEANOR ROOSEVELT**

Child's Play

Response-ability is a high-Self divine gift, part of our true nature. However, like a muscle it still requires exercise to grow strong. If the gift of response-ability isn't nourished when we are young, the low-self ego becomes dominant and, focused on the external, automatically falls into blame. 'You made me do that' is the childhood mantra that is all too often carried over into adulthood. Children who miss the lesson of responsibility become adults who are trapped in a self-made prison, saying to themselves: 'I can't help it, it's not my fault, it's just the way I am.'

> If you don't like something change it; if you can't change it, change the way you think about it.
>
> MARY ENGELBREIT

We started teaching our daughter Shanti about response-ability when she was about three by playing the 'choices game'. It can be a tough game to play especially when I'm asking her to eat her broccoli. ('I could choose ice-cream, Daddy, or chocolate.') Children lack the experience to know what is best for them and are dependent on adults for guidance until they are wiser.

Part of learning response-ability is to understand that some things lie outside of our immediate control. However, we can find a deeper level of *acceptance* by choosing our *response* to those things – choosing how to feel about them.

'Now please eat your broccoli and choose to like it!'

True-Self Freedom

When I was young I couldn't wait to leave what I saw as the restriction of school and be free. It took me some years to discover that you only truly achieve freedom by staying in school and learning the lessons of life. In the great school of life there are many levels with countless lessons to be learned. The lessons of life are not formal but rather natural and we learn by way of life-experience. Both the good and the so-called bad things have

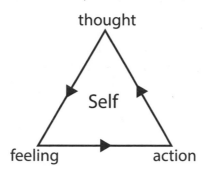

The thought-feeling-action cycle

something to teach us, if we are open to learning. However, if we don't *accept* the situation, if we are busy blaming, making excuses and justifying our actions, then we don't learn the lesson, which means we don't move up to the next level of true-Self happiness, peace and abundance.

Life is a school where the lesson is repeated as many times as required. Unfortunately, some people spend their entire lives never learning certain key lessons. They repeat the same old mistakes over and over, only each time the pain is increased.

The low self lacks real will and is instead governed by habits. Only the high Self has true will and is able to make 'consciously aware choices'. Practise choosing your response, of thought, feeling and action, on the little things, the petty annoyances of daily life and, like building a muscle, you will increase your power to choose when it comes to the really big things that lie outside our immediate control, such as relationships. Exercise your will, and it will gradually grow to an iron will and with it will come the deep inner freedom of your true Self.

Choices, Choices, Choices

Being *irresponsible* is a choice made from low-level consciousness; a choice that's made without consideration, without thinking things through, or sometimes with no real thought at all.

Often our low self sees responsibility not as a gift but as a punishment. We tell our self 'I have to', which actually implies that we have no choice. And we fix opinions about the external world which begin to become rules and judgements on anyone who doesn't abide by them. The low self uses responsibility as blame. 'It's your responsibility' is often meant and heard as 'it's your fault'. The 'blame game' is one we learn and start playing young. If it's rewarded it becomes a strong habit that we carry through life.

> When you blame others, you give up your power to change.
> **Dr Robert Anthony**

> The strongest principle of growth lies in the human choice.
> **George Eliot**

While our high Self is fluid and responsive, our low self is rigid and reactive. Choices made from our low self often become set-in beliefs, outlooks and opinions, regardless of the shifting reality around us. We cast judgements on others, and believe life should fit into a fixed mould. Without acceptance, there is no room for anything that sits apart from our opinion, beyond our philosophy or outside of our box.

In contrast, high-Self response-ability carries a pro-active attitude and an awareness that we are free at our deepest inner level, and therefore always have a choice in each and every moment. Through the qualities of balance and purpose, true-Self response-ability takes another step and seeks to make the right choice, in alignment with our values, and for the highest good of all. The acceptance of responsibility is yet another groove in the master key that sets us free.

Mind the Gap

When we do not choose peace and accept our self we become trapped in low self-esteem. Our ego's need for approval means we invariably crave some form of acceptance from others. We constantly try to match the picture that our partner, family or society holds up, whether it's the best fit for us or not.

Seeking acceptance from others causes us to act in ways we think we should, rather than simply being our true Self. The more we spiral down into our low self the greater the gap between high Self, who we really are, the 'I am' and our low self, who we think we need to be, the 'I should'.

> Tension is who you think you should be. Relaxation is who you are.
> **CHINESE PROVERB**

Sometimes we feel secure and show up in life as our true Self, 'I am', and other times when we feel insecure we fall into the trap of needing acceptance.

In the gap between our high Self and low self, the 'I am' and 'I should', lie all the different levels of incongruence and falseness of not being true to our Self. In the gap lies all neurosis, nervousness and uncertainty; all unease and discomfort.

The greater the gap the more the suffering we experience. Begin now to draw your self together over the bridge of self-acceptance by answering these questions:

◆ What causes you the most tension or stress?

◆ What do you make excuses for, need to defend, justify or be right about?

◆ What are you embarrassed about or ashamed of, what do you feel you need to hide or even lie about?

Think about them *now*.

It was in asking such searching questions that I saw aspects of my low self that I realized I was ashamed of, resisting, but still carrying with me.

Sometimes, we are very happy being a certain way with one group of people, but very uncomfortable being that way with another. Recently someone on my workshop justified their action by telling me that 'I choose not to smoke around my kids because I don't want them to pick up the habit.' While the intention was noble, one of the side-effects was that this person was still telling themselves, deep down, that a part of them was wrong.

We will never truly be free until we accept our low self and move on. The things that we resist about our self are things we are not at peace with. We therefore don't want to acknowledge them and block them from our mind. We must practise acceptance with our self to see past our ego. Then, by focusing beyond, we become who we most choose to be.

Look again at your answers to the questions above. What's the common thread? What are they showing you about your self that you've been unaware of, but could choose to accept, make peace with, and move beyond towards your true Self?

Judge Not

The spirit of our high Self is acceptance. The nature of our low self is resistance. And when these qualities are combined in our true Self we become discerning. To be discerning is not the same as judging. Discernment sees clearly and accepts the true nature of life, a situation or person, whereas judging makes it 'right' or 'wrong' in our opinion. When we judge our self, another or life, we do not really define, we simply demonstrate that we have not grown out of casting judgements, and in the process creating resistance, thereby stopping new growth.

> When we focus on clarifying what is being observed, felt, and needed rather than on diagnosing and judging, we discover the depth of our own compassion.
> **MARSHALL B ROSENBERG**

Freeing our self from judgement doesn't mean we ignore, turn a blind eye to or passively excuse; we simply stop making it right or wrong. We accept that mistakes happen, and can become learning if we are open; that life works in ways we don't always understand at first. And that everyone is on their own journey learning their own lessons, in their own way and in their own time.

Whenever we want to point out the splinter in another's eye we would do well to look first for the log in our own. One of the greatest reflections in life comes from our relationships. Look in the mirror of those about you to see who you are in response to them. You will see aspects of your relationship with your self, your positive accepting high Self as well as your negative rejecting low self.

On occasions I've felt deeply resentful of some-one who I feel has failed in some way, yet at the same time I've been completely blind to the same or sim-ilar behaviour and failings in some aspect of my self.

Practise acceptance of your self and you will naturally stop judging others. Only when we are great with our Self do we treat others in a great way. There is a story of a woman who took her child to see Gandhi and asked him, 'Will you tell my child to stop eating sugar?' She was told to come back in two weeks. When she returned Gandhi said to her son, 'Stop eating sugar.' The woman was puzzled and asked, 'Why could you not have told him two weeks ago?' Gandhi replied, 'Because it took me two weeks to stop taking sugar myself.'

The Golden Rule

Everything is connected to everything else, and therefore, whatever we do to another person, we are in some way doing to our self. This is one of the fundamental truths echoed throughout the ages, the golden rule of All.

In the Wiccan Rede we hear it as: 'An it harm none, do what ye will.'

> He who has learned to disagree without being disagreeable has discovered the most valuable secret of a diplomat.
> **ROBERT ESTABROOK**

> When you point the finger of blame, remember that three of your other fingers are pointing back at your self.
> **NATIVE AMERICAN PROVERB**

> There is little room left for wisdom when one is full of judgement.
> **MALCOLM HEIN**

> If your heart acquires strength, you will be able to remove blem-ishes from others without thinking evil of them.
> **MAHATMA GANDHI**

While in Buddhism the message is: 'Hurt not others with that which pains your self.'

Matthew 7:12 says: 'So in everything, do to others what you would have them do to you, for this sums up the Law and the Prophets.'

Confucianism expresses it in this way: 'Is there any one maxim which ought to be acted upon throughout one's whole life; surely the maxim of loving kindness is such. Do not unto others what you would not they should do unto you.'

Judaism tells us: 'What is hurtful to your self do not to your fellow man. That is the whole of the Torah and the remainder is but commentary. Go learn it.'

Hinduism instructs: 'This is the sum of duty: do naught to others which if done to thee, would cause thee pain.'

And in Islam the message is: 'No one of you is a believer until he loves for his brother what he loves for himself.'

Jainism states: 'In happiness and suffering, in joy and grief, we should regard all creatures as we regard our own self, and should therefore refrain from inflicting upon others such injury as would appear undesirable to us if inflicted upon ourselves.'

Sikhism says: 'As thou deemest thyself, so deem others. Then shalt thou become a partner in Heaven.'

The Tao informs us: 'Regard your neighbour's gain as your own gain: and regard your neighbour's loss as your own loss.'

And finally, in Zoroastrianism, one of the oldest religions in the world, we hear: 'That nature only is good when it shall not do unto another whatever is not good for its own self.'

Let Go and Let God

Choosing our response from our high Self, in acceptance to the flow of life, our relationships, situations and circumstance, allows us to be responsive, reflective and reverent.

Let go of all your expectations and judgements and just be in the moment, rather than focusing on how you think things should be. Choose to do a thing, or choose not to. But don't do it begrudgingly, with a bad attitude. Accept the thing, embrace it, or reject it and move away from it.

Life is always changing. The current is constantly shifting and the flow dividing. Our ability to be responsive to the unexpected allows us to navigate the various steams of life towards our desired destination. By practising acceptance we flow around the barriers of life to manifest our true Self's desires in perfect ways.

The goals that we set for our self become like beacons of light that we steer towards on our quest The tide may turn many times, and the sea change, but always through acceptance we can choose our response, the set of the sail, and make good progress even against the force of the wind.

Life is on your side and lending a hand. God, the universe, life, wants you to succeed. If it were otherwise there would be no existence.

Learn to accept gifts and compliments. In the past, whenever someone told me they'd enjoyed my presentation, or praised my work, I would always respond by putting my self down and saying, 'Oh it's nothing really.' It took me some time to see that I felt unworthy of the praise and didn't really value my self. I have so often sold my self short, undervaluing my self and thereby my work. 'No, go on, have it', I would say when someone was offering money for one of my books. Part of me would justify it by saying 'I like to give a gift.' However, another part of me was giving it away because I felt worthless, and therefore felt that my work couldn't be worth much either.

Once I was asked to run some workshops for a large banking organization. The director in charge was so pleased with my first pilot workshop that he told me to put my charges up. But I couldn't accept the compliment and spluttered; 'Oh, I couldn't possibly.' To which he replied 'OK, have it your way' and walked off.

The pain of contemplating the lesson over and over in the following months helped me realize truths about my self and I started practising acceptance by simply saying 'thank you' to every compliment and gift, criticism or challenge that came my way.

Resistance Is Futile

What we resist, in our self and life, persists. To resist something is to push against it, which means we are giving our energy to it. The deeper our level of resistance the greater the level of energy burned and the more it drains us.

In contrast, when we accept a person, situation or quality of self, for what it is, we stop dwelling on *it* and instead begin to focus again on our goals – where we are going, what we are doing and who we choose to become as a person.

Let go of the need to impress others, control situations or resist aspects of your self and life, and you begin to flow with the moment.

> The key is to not resist or rebel against emotions or to try to get around them by devising all sorts of tricks; but to accept them directly, as they are.
>
> **Takahisa Kora**

> I have learned that resistance is a pointer, and that what I have resisted most is usually also the true direction of my life.
>
> **Nick Williams**

In any given moment, regardless of situation or circumstance, we can raise our awareness of our self and become more conscious. We can question our feelings. And because we are aware, we can choose our response rather than react from old habit-patterns. In so doing, each day we live a little more from the qualities of our true Self. This practice of raising awareness, acknowledging feelings and making conscious choices gradually causes an upward spiral of self-evolution, inner freedom and enlightenment.

Accepting our high Self is just as important as accepting our low self. Many people deny their own greatness and cast a shadow over their own light. Regularly people tell me that they want to live a more meaningful life but don't know what their purpose is. After talking with them for a time I often find that they do know their purpose but are resisting it because they also fear it in some way.

In truth, it is only by accepting our high Self, our low self and our life that we are able to integrate, become whole and gain the complete freedom of our true Self.

— ◆ —

IN ESSENCE

The essence to remember and live from in this chapter is:

Accept your self
and your Self and the
kingdom is yours.

Creating Your Self Map

Ask your self these freeing questions:

◆ What most annoys you about people and life?

◆ What does this show you that you have not fully accepted in your self?

◆ What would your high Self choose now?

Step 5 – High-Self Attitudes

Mental Attitudes

Continue to fill in your high-Self mandala by connecting with a positive high-Self moment, either an actual event from your past or by imagining how you would choose to be in your ideal life. This time observe your empowering mental attitudes. For example, are you optimistic, inquisitive, focused or positive?

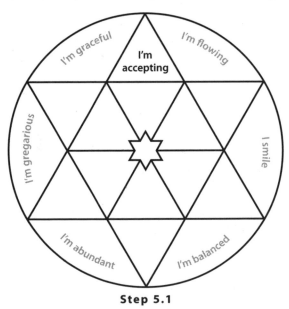

Step 5.1

Remember to consider your already stated mental habit and think about what attitude might empower it. Then write your statement, as before, using pen and the present tense, in the top triangle.

Emotional Attitudes

Next, observe your attitudes with regard to the emotional aspects of your high Self. When being your high Self are you open, happy, loving or joyful? Again, remember to consider your existing high-Self habit statement, and place your insight in the next triangle round.

Physical Attitudes

Now, staying connected to your high Self, consider your main attitudes to your physical self. Are you balanced, honouring and nurturing in your attitude towards your body? Trust your intuition or review the freeing questions for inspiration, then write your statement in the next triangle.

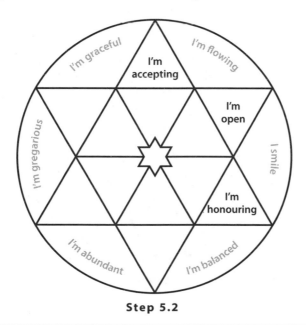

Step 5.2

Material Attitudes

What about your material attitudes when being your high Self? Are you, for instance, balanced in your finances, thoughtful and fair? Capture your insight in the appropriate triangle in pen and the present tense.

Social Attitudes

Next consider your high-Self attitudes socially. Are you affectionate, respectful, accepting or open? Capture your insight, in pen and the present tense, in the next triangle.

Spiritual Attitudes

Finally, observe or imagine and then record your spiritual attitudes when being your high Self. Are you grateful, hopeful, centred or aware? Write your observation in the last triangle.

Step 5.3

Chapter 6

Self-love

Love, Love, Love

Love is all there is. Love is who you truly are. Love is the glue that binds *you* together. Love is the place of self-integration – where you become whole, create whole relationships and live a whole life. There can be no true connection to Spirit, pursuit of purpose, happiness, peace or abundance without love. Love is the creative force of the universe felt in us as the prime emotion. Love is the grandest gift you can give, and the greatest gift you have already received, yours by divine right. At the core of your being, you *are* love, and can be in love, simply and freely by choosing to live from your true Self.

> Love is a choice you make from moment to moment.
> **BARBARA DE ANGELIS**
>
> Love doesn't make the world go round. Love is what makes the ride worthwhile.
> **FRANKLIN JONES**

Choose to be in love with your Self; be in love with others; be in love with life.

Highs and Lows

The high Self, being connected to our essence, is love, pure and simple. It is our natural, unconditional, ever-present, radiant source of complete comfort, core nourishment and true wellbeing. There are many shades of love that colour our world, such as romantic or passionate love, friendship or platonic love, love for family, maternal love, fraternal love for humanity, love of a thing, love of life and love of God. However, 'the greatest love of all', as Whitney Houston sang, is inside of me, and you, and everyone else. Learning to love your self is the greatest love of all because it is the gift that creates love for all else, and without love from the high Self to the low self there can be no true love for anything or anyone.

High-Self love, that is, 'true love', is born of appreciation. It is complete, asks nothing and gives everything. It is an outpouring of purely positive energy from our divine essence.

In contrast, the low self, being born of separation, craves the complete comfort of true love, but when denied or lacking in love, eventually becomes bitter and hateful, both towards itself and towards others.

Being judgemental, the low self is always finding fault with some aspect of itself and life. It doesn't really like itself. And the more lacking in love the low self feels, the more discomfort it carries, and the lower it falls. Dislike becomes self-loathing and self-hatred, sinking still further into various forms of self-harm and even total self-destruction. All this can not only be imposed within the self, but can also be reflected out on others in the form of prejudice, persecution and brutality. Whether inwardly or outwardly, the ultimate fall of the low self results in some form of self-destruction, perhaps even in suicide or murder.

> **Friendship with one's self is all important, because without it one cannot be friends with anyone else in the world.**
> **ELEANOR ROOSEVELT**

I'll Love You If...

While the high Self, like a baby, loves unconditionally, the low self, having been shaped by its environment, places expectations and restrictions on love. If these are not met, love can turn into bitterness and resentment.

Almost everyone will grow up experiencing conditional love to some degree; 'I'll love you if...' is the basic message we receive. Even it is not directly said, we learn subconsciously through our life-experience that sometimes we see, hear and feel love, and at other times we don't. Many people will declare their love for another person, and even mean it when they say it, but because they don't truly love their self, they become the slave of their cravings, moods and habits, and are unable to be the person they would choose to be for the other.

Often we grow up confusing lust or longing for love. Feelings of attraction and physical connection to another, no matter how wonderful and powerful, are not true love. They are signs of the collapse of the ego's boundaries or walls – the thrill of vulnerability as we allow our self to become close and intimate with another.

The more *unconditional* the love we receive, the more nourished our high Self becomes and we shine brightly. However, the more *conditional* the love we receive, the more it feeds our low self and the ego becomes dominant.

When we love from our ego we are invariably reactive and easily caused to fling cruel words or perform hurtful actions if our expectations or gestures of love are not met. It's that bitter snipe in the heat of an argument that flies like poison to the heart of another; it's that smack on your child that you wish hadn't happened but you can't take back. It's that negative self-destructive habit that not only wrecks your own life but also brings grief to those around you.

In truth, while often uncomfortable to acknowledge, it is undeniable that:

> *You cannot genuinely love anyone else*
> *more than you truly love your self.*

Love Is All

Ultimately, everything comes from the One; and in like manner all emotion comes from just one core emotion: love. Just as darkness is the absence of light, so fear is the absence of love.

Hatred, like all other negative emotions, is simply what's left when love is missing.

People who become trapped in low-self emotions are often referred to as having a 'narcissistic personality' – they are highly self-centred. The term comes from the ancient Greek myth about Narcissus, a handsome youth who rejected the nymph Echo and was doomed to fall in love with his own reflection in a pool.

When we fall in love with the reflection of our low self we become trapped, looking into a stagnant pool of heavy emotions; we become vain, bitter, and egotistical. The ego's need to be 'the best' at everything, and the dread of appearing wrong, stupid or incompetent, creates a self-centred snob who needs to believe they are better in some way, superior, elite and often indifferent to the plight of others. However, underneath all the various masks of protection they still crave love.

> Fear less, hope more; eat less, chew more; whine less, breathe more; talk less, say more; love more, and all good things will be yours.
>
> SWEDISH PROVERB

Man or Monkey, We All Crave Comfort

In a famous experiment, Dr Harry Harlow of the University of Wisconsin removed infant rhesus monkeys from their mothers and placed them in a cage with a choice of two substitute mothers. One was made of cold wire with a feeding bottle where the nipple would normally be, while the other was made of warm comfortable cloth, but with no feeding nipple.

In essence Harlow wanted to discover which the monkeys would choose: food or love. The experiment showed that even though there was no feeding nipple, the baby monkeys chose the love or comfort of the cloth mother, and only when really hungry, and then just for short periods, did they leave to feed from the cold wire monkey.

When older, the monkeys were timid, disturbed by the presence of other monkeys, extremely fearful of anything unusual and spent most of their time upset. As parents they took little interest in their own offspring and were often abusive. Because they had no experience of being reared themselves, they lacked knowledge of how to care for their own babies and showed little or no empathy towards them.

In contrast, other monkeys that had been reared by their natural mothers, sought out the love and attention they needed. Often, the behaviour of the mothers would change as they responded to their young and became more nurturing.

Parenting, it would seem, is partly learned from our parents and partly from our children.

> When we feel love and kindness toward others, it not only makes them feel loved and cared for, but it helps us also to develop inner happiness and peace.
> THE DALAI LAMA

Wild Child

Children need love like roses need rain. Just as a lack of nutrients leads to physical deficiencies, so a lack of genuine love results in emotional blocks and behavioural problems. An unloved child, unstimulated, uncared for, does not develop in the same way as a child who is interacted with, caressed and unconditionally loved. Regardless of what gifts we are born with, to become our true Self will require love or nurture to enhance our nature.

The true-life cases of 'feral children' who have been lost or abandoned and raised by animals show that they do not always make it off of all fours, learn a language or develop a full range of emotions, particularly high-Self emotions such as love, empathy and compassion.

It shows that we do not develop our true humanity unless we are shown true humanity. To some degree, children raised by humans, but not shown genuine love and compassion, develop similarly low levels of humanity. The more we descend into our low self the more animalistic we become, unaware and driven by our low-self cravings for comfort.

What's Wrong with Me?

When a young child loses a parent or parents, whether through death, separation or simply to the TV, work or the pub, the child feels unloved and forms a deep sense of abandonment. At an early age children are unable to reason away or rationalize this loss and generally conclude that it must be because *they* are not good enough in some way, not *worth* hanging on to, not worth the attention.

This conclusion is usually reached at a subconscious level and as the child grows older they become less and less aware that this deep-seated outlook is subtly but powerfully shaping their *attitudes*, *behaviour* and thereby their *life*. If the outlook, picture or belief that we hold is one of being ignored, abandoned or abused by a significant other, then it becomes the drama that we play out again and again as we attract people into our life who we subconsciously know will mistreat, leave or harm us.

Years ago a good friend of mine continually returned to an abusive relationship, much to the frustration of the people who cared for her. At the time I didn't understand that her feeling of being 'worthless' was driving her to subconsciously punish herself in various ways. Only when she reached a crisis point and mentally broke down – *broke through the mask of ego* – did she behold the magnificence of her true Self and glimpse the insight that she was truly worthwhile. That was the turning point, as it is for millions of others in all manner of situations. She made a stand for her true Self and began to move on with her life.

> People are like stained-glass windows. They sparkle and shine when the sun is out, but when the darkness sets in, their true beauty is revealed only if there is a light from within.
>
> **ELISABETH KÜBLER-ROSS**

The Guilt Game

While most relationships are not physically abusive, they are often mentally and emotionally harmful or draining – a slow poisoning of our self through bitter thoughts and soured feelings. Of all the low-self toxic emotions that bring us down, *guilt* is the most self-destructive. Guilt is driven by a belief or outlook that *you* are *wrong* in some way: not that something you have done is wrong, but that you as a person are wrong. Once the deep-seated belief that you are wrong has been established it can affect every area and aspect of your life for years to come.

If something good should happen – if you should attract the right partner; land the right work, bring some good fortune into your life – then *guilt* tells you to make sure you mess it up, because deep down at an unconscious level the unspoken feeling and command is: 'You don't deserve it.'

Nothing exists without a purpose. When guilt is balanced with high-Self emotions, it plays its proper role as part of our self-control system. A healthy or balanced sense of guilt helps us to learn the lessons of life. Without it we might commit the most atrocious acts, even against those we are closest to.

Unfortunately, not only is guilt a natural self-control system, it is also a powerful way of controlling others, which is precisely why parents and children, leaders and religions have used it for thousands of years to get others to do want they want.

Most people, of course, are only casual guilt-trippers, while others are real masters, and some even have the equivalent of a black-belt in guilt. 'No, you just go on; enjoy yourself, why don't you? Don't worry about me; I'll be all right' is not the genuine message. The real emotion expressed through the tone of voice tells us the unspoken opinion and command which actually is, 'Don't enjoy yourself; feel bad, it's not fine by me; I think you are wrong.'

When confronted, guilt-trippers usually hide behind the mask of justification and denial: 'I'm only telling the truth. You should have done better; you knew we were all depending on you.' When pushed, they might even apply more guilt by feigning emotion and illness: 'You've made me so sad' they wail like children through crocodile tears, usually while coughing, limping or holding their head.

The Pain of Guilt

The natural self-control system of guilt is meant to work like a pain receptor. When you do something physically reckless, pain lets you know you are causing damage to your self. Likewise, when you are irresponsible in your life, the pain of guilt lets you know you are doing harm. Pain should only be fleeting, but when a child experiences excessive guilt focused on the self, they become conditioned to feel it always. Indeed, they need it, just like an addict needs a drug, and then the pain never goes away and they find reasons to feel guilty everywhere they go and in everything they do.

A child who grows up feeling something is wrong with them carries a heavy sense of guilt, and subconsciously moves towards situations and people that they can feel guilty about. Guilt-catchers unwittingly attract guilt-givers, and vice versa. The dominant attitude of the guilt-tripper is 'You've made me.' Instead of choosing their thoughts, feelings and behaviours, they surrender their power and happiness to circumstance and other people. They play the victim and give up their responsibility which is replaced instead by blame and excuses ('Now look what you've made me do', such a person might say, 'you've made me lose my temper') as they play out a negative dance of dependent self-destruction, attracting even greater levels of guilt, pain and sadness into their lives.

Forgive Your Low Self

Throughout my own childhood, my teens and into my early adult life I carried a deep sense of guilt stemming from a belief that there was something wrong with me. Not that you would have noticed, as I buried it under a mask of cockiness, arrogance and boasting.

When my life crashed at around age 30, the mask was dislodged enough for me to glimpse the horrible truth: I was living a lie. Not only was I riddled to my core with guilt, I was also using it on others to get my own way. Up till then, I had been completely blind to it.

Fortunately, I discovered personal development and Spirit around the same time and so began an ongoing journey of seeking to become my true Self. I took a giant step forward in making peace with my self and letting go of guilt the day I realized a simple but fundamental truth:

Everyone does the best they can with what they have – and that includes their start in life.

It's encoded into our genes to strive and be all we can be. However, we don't all receive the amount of love and attention we need to nurture our nature and become the person we are capable of being, regardless of the prosperity of our parents or community.

> It is our own heart, and not other men's opinions, that forms our true honour.
> SAMUEL TAYLOR COLERIDGE

Feeling guilty for not measuring up to someone else's expectations or, for that matter, your own simply empowers your low self by feeding negative energy to it, saying 'I'm not good enough.' The internal comment eventually becomes a literal command to the subconscious, thereby keeping you stuck in a small place, constantly feeling bad about your self.

Guilt Free

The journey of true self-love and being 'guilt free' begins with *acceptance* and gradually grows into *forgiveness*; first of your self by acknowledging that you have done your best, with the start you had, even in those situations you may not be particularly proud of; and secondly of others: understanding that they have done their best with the start they had.

There is a tendency in some people, as they realize that their negative outlooks, attitudes and behaviours stem from the influences of their childhood, to blame their parents for their shortcomings. But this does not help us to be free from guilt and actually creates new negative emotions of bitterness, blame and resentment, which further empower our low self. In truth no one consciously chooses to be either a catcher or giver of guilt, or any other negative emotion; it is something that we learn, usually from our parents, who in turn learnt it from their parents, and so on.

As Jesus instructed from the Cross:

Forgive them for they know not what they are doing.

LUKE 23:34

Forgive everyone and everything. Forgiveness is not really something you do for another person, although they may receive a blessing from it; it is something that you primarily do for your self. It is self-healing.

Simply by choosing to *let go* of any bitterness, guilt or resentment you hold, even without anyone else knowing of it, you begin self-healing and the process of self-integration; at essence, you are accepting your self – all of you.

Begin by forgiving the little things. Practise holding the outlook that people rarely do stuff on purpose to annoy you; there is no real conspiracy in life; the traffic jam didn't come just to ruin your day. By forgiving on the little things we build our forgiveness muscle, reintegrate our true Self, and become stronger at forgiving the big things.

Forgiveness will not change your past, but it will enlarge your future. Without it you can't move on. The more anger, bitterness or resentment you carry in your heart about the past, the less capable of love, compassion and empathy you are in the present.

Show Some Respect

Just as there can be no true self-love without forgiveness, likewise there can be no real forgiveness without respect. True respect requires an appreciation of our self, life and others – an awareness that everyone and everything has a natural divine right to exist; that all are part of the whole, just as waves are part of the ocean.

As with acceptance, forgiveness and love, respect also begins on the inside with respect for our self. The paradox, however, is that when we fall into being our low self we have no real respect for our self but want it from others. 'Show some respect' is a common comment that stems from an inner unseen reality of 'because I don't really respect my self'. True respect comes from authentic self-appreciation; a feeling of self-worth; that you have lived to the best of your ability with the resources or start that you had and in alignment with the beliefs and values you've formed.

An Attitude of Gratitude

To say 'no' to what we don't want we must learn to say 'yes' to what we do want. It is not possible to hold both a negative and a positive thought in our mind at the same time. Focusing on what is right prevents us from dwelling too long on what is wrong.

> When a deep injury is done to us, we never recover until we forgive.
> **ALAN PATON**

> He who cannot forgive others destroys the bridge over which he himself must pass.
> **GEORGE HERBERT**

> To carry a grudge is like being stung to death over and over by the same bee.
> **WILLIAM WALTON**

This is an important lesson for a number of reasons, not least of which is that our subconscious, like universal consciousness, do not make judgements about the quality or focus of our thoughts. They simply respond to them by starting to create and attract whatever we think about most often.

Proverbs 23:7 tells us:

As he thinks within himself
so he is.

Choose to be grateful in your heart for what you have received and what you hope to receive in the future, and you automatically focus your mind on the positive. By focusing on what's right with your self and life you find the energy and heart to heal what's not, which moves you closer to being your true Self.

Whatever we focus on, good or bad, grows in our awareness, becomes a dominant outlook and thereby a command to our subconscious to make it so. Self-sabotage is an unconscious game that starts with thoughts, focused on what we don't want, empowered through feelings of fear, and then delivered through negative behaviour.

Choose to see the good, or god, in your self. Hold a positive focus on what's best about your self and you will blossom. Focus on love and you become loving and lovable. Be in love with your self, develop genuine self appreciation, be grateful, and you bring your self into bloom.

Self-talk

Every thought we think is the equivalent of a command to our subconscious, super-conscious or universal consciousness about our self and the quality of life we create, attract and experience. The thoughts that we repeat over and over, particularly those that we

> Treat people as if they were what they ought to be and you help them to become what they are capable of being.
>
> **GOETHE**

> Self-respect is the fruit of discipline: the sense of dignity grows with the ability to say no to oneself.
>
> **ABRAHAM HESCHEL**

speak out loud, become dominant commands. Most often the positive and negative simply cancel each other out. Occasionally things do not go as we'd hoped and we fall into a torrent of self-destructive language – 'What's the use? I'll never be able to do it. Why do I always get things wrong?' – thereby issuing the wrong commands and unwittingly sinking even lower.

Say Something Nice

Though the low self spits out words of hate, the high Self flows with the language of love. By saying something great to our self we are able to build it up, bring out our greatness and empower our true Self.

> Celebrate what you want to see more of.
> **THOMAS PETERS**
>
> Gratitude is heaven itself.
> **WILLIAM BLAKE**
>
> Every word that you express will return to you.
> **CHRISTIAN LARSON**

Early on in my personal development journey I accepted a challenge from my mentor to demonstrate self-appreciation. My task seemed simple: first thing every morning I was to walk confidently up to the bathroom mirror, look my self in the eye, and five times, with as much positive feeling as I could muster, repeat the magic words: 'I like my self.'

It was so hard that at first I couldn't do it. It simply wasn't the truth for me in how I felt about my self. My low self had become dominant, and the mantra of low self that I had been quietly saying was: 'I don't like my self.'

The first time I finally uttered: 'I like my self', it was through gritted teeth, forcing the words over my feelings. However, as if by magic, by the fifth time I said it I had a big cheesy grin on my face and a warm glow in my heart. The thought 'I like my self' had triggered the release of positive chemicals into my system, such as serotonin, that gave me a physical feeling of well-being.

'I like my self' is the message that creates the reality of self-love and, through it, self-integration. A verbalized thought gains in vibration, builds in power and increases your inner energy. It took me many years of saying, 'I like my self' before I came to say, and mean; 'I love my self.'

In 1934 Dale Wimbrow penned 'The Guy in the Glass', as a response to a young man's questions about whether living a life of integrity was really as important as achieving results. The poem gets straight to the heart of self-love and has a fundamental message for us all:

> When you get what you want in your struggle for
>   pelf,
> And the world makes you King for a day,
> Then go to the mirror and look at yourself,
> And see what that guy has to say.
>
> For it isn't your Father, or Mother, or Wife,
> Who judgement upon you must pass.
> The feller whose verdict counts most in your life
> Is the guy staring back from the glass.
>
> He's the feller to please, never mind all the rest,
> For he's with you clear up to the end,
> And you've passed your most dangerous,
>   difficult test
> If the guy in the glass is your friend.
>
> You may be like Jack Horner and 'chisel' a plum,
> And think you're a wonderful guy,
> But the man in the glass says you're only a bum
> If you can't look him straight in the eye.
>
> You can fool the whole world down the pathway
>   of years,
> And get pats on the back as you pass,
> But your final reward will be heartaches and tears
> If you've cheated the guy in the glass.

– ◆ –

IN ESSENCE

The essence to remember and live from in this chapter is:

At the core of your being
you are love, you only need
to remember it.

Creating Your Self Map

Ask your self these freeing questions:

◆ What do you love most in your self?

◆ What are you most grateful for in your life?

◆ What is the *least* loving thing you say to your self?

Step 6 – High-Self Outlooks

By this point in creating your high-Self mandala you may find the same quality showing up in different life areas. As before, this simply indicates your strong positive qualities, which you can state more than once, or gain even greater benefit by searching deeper to find what sits beyond.

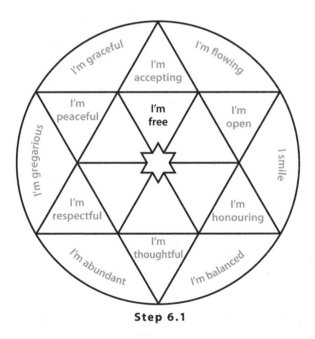

Step 6.1

Mental Outlook

Connect with a high-Self moment or imagine being the way that you choose to be, and notice your main outlooks. Do you see your Self as essentially free, open and aware?

Choose a quality that feels right, trust your intuition, or review the freeing questions for help, then state your insight in the top inner triangle, as per the example.

Emotional Outlook

Now flow on through and observe your high-Self opinion or outlook of your self emotionally. Do you like and love your self? When being your high Self, are you blissful, compassionate and heart-led?

Physical Outlook

Next, picture how you see your self physically. When being your high Self, do you see your body as being worthwhile,

Step 6.2

special, perfect or priceless? As before, write your statement in pen and the present tense in the appropriate triangle, as in the example on page 131.

Material Outlook

Now consider your material and financial outlook. Do you have a picture of your self as prosperous and abundant, the conscious creator of your desires?

Social Outlook

What is your social outlook? Do you see your self as connected, inclusive, interdependent, appreciative, belonging?

Spiritual Outlook

And finally, observe your outlook when being your high Self spiritually. Are you divine, eternal, One?

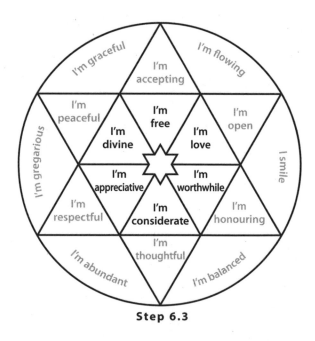

Step 6.3

Part Three

Action

Chapter 7

Self-actualization

By Thought, Word and Deed We Make Our World

Life begets life. Creation is self-creative. From the subatomic iteration of energies that create particles, to the cooperation of cells that form our bodies, to the interaction of species that produce ecosystems, the very act of living is a creative process.

As with the collective so with the individual, for each of us is constantly actualizing our self and creating our personal world. Like waves, the energy we individually generate through our thoughts, words and deeds interacts with the collective ocean of life, thereby giving shape and form to our own experience of reality.

Sometimes our thoughts, feelings and actions spring from positive conscious intentions and we create our dreams. And sometimes they are unconsciously or negatively driven and result in us attracting our worst nightmares. However, always, and in all ways, for better or worse, whether we are aware of it or not, it is the trinity of our thoughts, words and deeds, or *outlooks*, *attitudes* and *actions*, which, like a many-linked chain of cause and effect, unfolds to shape our world.

Self-actualization is the process of *consciously creating* our self and, through it, steering our life. The term 'actualization' is derived from the word 'actual', which in turn comes from the Latin *actus*, meaning an 'act' or 'a doing'. Actualization then is not just imagined or felt; it is 'made real' through action.

Our *thoughts* are the initial sparks that light the fire of our intentions, goals or purpose; our *feelings* are the lingering fuels that keep the fire burning; and together they heat the steam that powers the piston of our *actions* – whereby we physically manifest our life. While thoughts are fleeting, feelings linger and actions become anchored in habit. At each stage, thought, feeling and action, our power to actualize our self and create our desired reality is magnified.

Highs and Lows

Actualization from the high Self is the path of becoming all that you can be, the path of consciously choosing your thoughts, feelings and actions and, through them, living a purposeful life that reflects your authentic heartfelt desires.

In contrast, when we live from our low self we are most often *unconscious* and *reactive* in our actualization. We are generally unaware that our repeated thoughts and words have become our beliefs, that our most frequent feelings have solidified into attitudes, that our regular actions or deeds have become habits resulting in irresponsible behaviour and unwanted or sometimes disastrous consequences.

Goethe said:

> Action may not always bring happiness;
> but there is no happiness without action.
> **BENJAMIN DISRAELI**
>
> The smallest act of kindness is worth more than the greatest intention.
> **KAHLIL GIBRAN**

> To think is easy. To act is difficult.
> To act as one thinks is the most difficult of all.

Too often the least of us keeps the best of us down. When we live from our low self we tend to think and feel one way, but act in another. And, not keeping our word to our self and others, we live a life of disharmony. Just thinking good on its own does not really create true goodness. Neither does feeling good. Only

> Happiness is when what you think, what you say, and what you do are in harmony.
> **MAHATMA GANDHI**
>
> Be changed and the world around you begins to change.
> **GERALD EPSTEIN**

by thinking, feeling and doing good do we create true goodness, for our self and others. One of the greatest causes of unhappiness comes from believing in one thing, while saying the opposite, and doing something completely different.

Pull Your *Self* Together

Each of us is a complex combination of thoughts, feelings and actions, bound together by a web of intention. Thought without action is futile. Action without thought is misguided, and either one without feeling is weak. Only when our thoughts, feelings and actions are in alignment with each other and led by our heart with a pure intention are we our true Self and thereby work wonders in our world.

The way of the Self Mapping system is to hold a conscious image of you being true to your high Self, in thought, word and deed, as often as possible, so as to grow your low self into that consciously chosen mould. By holding the intention to draw the threads of our self together, like strands of a rope, we form harmony, integrity and an inner cord of great strength by which we can pull our Self and self together.

In consistently living from our true Self, choosing a high-Self response to our low-self weaknesses and undesired circumstance, we begin to create unity of thought, word and deed, raise our self-esteem and gradually attract real magic into our lives.

Creature of Habit

All creatures form habit-patterns of thought, feeling and action; they are part of our self-guidance system and help us to flow through life without constant conscious effort. Habits are not the same as instincts, we are not born with them; they are learnt or conditioned. Most of our primary habits – walking, talking, eating, etc. – are picked up unconsciously at a young age through repetition.

Struggle, or 'energy through effort', is nature's way of strengthening. The butterfly must break free of the cocoon if it is to fly. Work the muscle and it grows strong. While we may not always enjoy it, struggle is a big part of how we learn and grow. Getting something wrong is often necessary in order for us to understand how to get it right.

The universe is always giving us feedback on how we can improve if we are open. To a child, falling over is often seen as part of the game in learning to stay balanced. During the period of writing this book my daughter Ayesha has grown from a baby to a toddler, learning many new things along the way. At first, everything required effort, mentally, emotionally and physically. However, now, even at her tender age, many of the things she once struggled with have become easy and automatic habit-patterns, which now allow her to focus on new challenges and reach for new heights.

> A life spent making mistakes is not only more honourable, but more useful than a life spent doing nothing.
> **GEORGE BERNARD SHAW**

To paraphrase the great Ralph Waldo Emerson:

That which we persist in becomes easier, not that the nature of the thing changes, but that we become more in our Self.

Unconscious Habits

Most people are unaware of their own personal habits, which are largely 'picked up' through our experience of life rather than consciously chosen. Sometimes habits become deeply held convictions that are passed on down the generations to become customs, rituals and even laws, long after their true meaning and purpose has been forgotten.

For example, saluting in the military is said to stem from a time when knights wore helmets with visors, which they would raise when approaching a friendly knight so as to be recognized. For some military people the habit of saluting has become so ingrained that they find it hard not to salute even when the situation doesn't call for it.

While our habits are intended to serve us, some really limit us, and if we are unconscious of them it's like playing Russian roulette: sooner or later we are going to shoot our self by doing something totally inappropriate.

I recently watched a reality TV programme where a family was filmed to help them see some of their unconscious habits. When the film was played back the parents couldn't believe the way they'd acted towards their children. Both the mother and the grandmother were horrified when they observed footage showing them force-feeding the children at mealtimes. The habit was originally formed by the grandmother and driven by her *belief* that 'You must eat all the food on your plate.' Her belief and the reflected habits where originally created from good intentions in a bygone time of hardship. The habit had been passed on down the generations, and was completely out of harmony with the present situation and needs of the children.

> **Habit is either the best of servants or the worst of masters.**
> NATHANIEL EMMONS

The child is father of the man.

Just One More

Before my conscious journey into personal development and search for my true Self I had run a disco and been a DJ for many years. At the end of a good night, when the lights came on and the music went off, the cry from the crowd on the dance floor would come: 'Just one more!' I delighted in turning the lights back off and the music right up for another last tune, at the end of which would come again the cry: 'Just one more!' On one particular occasion 'just one more' eventually took me an hour past closing time and into trouble with the authorities.

In like manner, 'just one more' is the lie our ego tells to our self when confronted with dropping a habit we know is bad for us, but that our low self has attached all manner of comfort to. While our true Self knows that we don't really want it, another part of us, our low self, craves the false comfort, and we end up pulling our self apart. The longer we continue to act from the habit, the stronger it grows and 'just one more' carries the habit way over time and into an addiction.

All of us will form habits that can become addictions. Such addictions might not be the obvious and common vices of smoking or drinking, but even dieting, and exercising. Too much of anything can be bad for you.

Addictions are driven by a hunger that always needs feeding. Sometimes we are conscious of our addictions and justify them with comments like, 'I just can't help myself – I keep on doing it.' At other times we are totally unconscious of our addictions and spend our life in denial: 'I don't do that.'

> **Habit is a cable; we weave a thread of it each day, and at last we cannot break it.**
> **HORACE MANN**

All low-self habit-patterns are invariably driven by the craving for comfort. Unfortunately, our low self attaches itself to false comforts that never truly satisfy and we are forever chasing the comfort dragon for 'just one more'.

That which we resist, give our energy to, persists. The hunger grows stronger as we crave the thing we feel is lacking. Sometimes we manage to overcome our urges and break free of the physical habit, but because the hunger for comfort still exists in our core, the ego simply finds another outlet for the craving and we form a new addiction.

> *Either you find your Self or you*
> *are enslaved by your self.*

In truth, it is only by living from our high Self, our natural source of complete comfort, where we are whole, and therefore crave nothing, that we ever truly satisfy the need of our low self. Then the old habits naturally drop away like dead wood from a living tree. We simply shed a skin we no longer fit in.

By Their Fruit

When I first met my partner, Sangeeta, she introduced me to a new saying: 'Water is wet and rocks are hard.' It took me a while to understand what she meant by it: that you must separate fact from fiction, and that *life* is the great teacher. If you want to see your self, look at what you are repeatedly experiencing, attracting or creating in your life. Let reality be the teacher that helps you to 'get real' about your *self* and life.

Often we will want to think of our self as being a certain way because low-self habits can be so unpleasant or painful to observe and acknowledge. We may profess to speak with an authentic voice and good heart, but as Matthew 7:16 states:

> By their fruit you will recognize them.

Within the course of a day we will think many different thoughts, some of which may be extremely noble. However, it is those that are entertained most often that become beliefs and thereby commands to our self and the universe. Likewise we may have a full range of emotions, but again it is those that are felt most often that charge the energy we put out into the world. Actions or behaviour are our densest level of interaction with life and therefore carry the greatest physically creative effect.

Do not waste your self in rejection, nor bark against the bad, but chant the beauty of the good.
EMERSON

Observation of life can help us to understand that effects happen with action, but not without it.
VINCE LOMBARDI

Habit of Choice

By exercising our free will we are able to break any habit-pattern at any link in the chain – mental, emotional, physical – and choose instead a different focus, feeling and thereby action. The easiest point to influence is *thought*; for once the power of feeling has been added the impulse to action is stronger.

> We must first make our habits, and then our habits make us.
> **JOHN DRYDEN**
>
> Excellence is a habit.
> **ARISTOTLE**

Make a stand for your true Self by defining and holding a picture of the 'best' you, and you thereby interrupt the pattern of old habits to break free. If we break old patterns, and consciously choose new ones, our habits begin to work for us and our low self evolves from unconscious dictator to noblest of supporters.

Self-help

One of great turning points in my life came when I lost everything – my marriage, home and possessions. Although I cried bitterly about my sorry situation, I also felt a new freedom, like a great weight had been lifted from me. I now count my self blessed for the experience, as through it I was led into the discovery of personal development and, by its faithful application, the creation of a new wonderful life.

I decided to put the philosophy of personal development (that by changing the attitude of your head and heart you can alter the conditions of your life) fully to the test. The first great physical change I noticed was in overcoming my reading difficulties. I felt a lifting of self-esteem at finally learning to read well and wanted to read everything. I chose, however, to focus on discovering more about self-help.

I speed-read more than a book a week, attended all the courses I could afford, and listened constantly to audio programmes. Gradually I noticed that the wisest of all the various teachings were in essence the same. Then one day I came across a statement:

There comes a point in each person's development where they would do well to pay less attention to the ideas and opinions of others, and more time in cultivating ideas and opinions of their own.

The statement stuck in my mind and kept repeating. I started noticing other statements that were saying the same thing in slightly different ways, like the Lao-Tzu quotation on this page.

I started to realize that no one can truly give you happiness; no one can give you hope or joy, confidence or belief. These are all things that we must do for our self. We are all playing a self-help game. Other people can help us learn the rules, but we must roll the dice. It is a limitation to surrender completely one's mind to any particular individual, no matter how enlightened; any system, however noble; any religion, however righteous. Listen to all of them, learn from some, but be your own council. All wisdom is within your self. The way is *your* way. Find it for your self.

> At the centre of your being you have the answer; you know who you are and you know what you want.
> **LAO-TZU**

> To know how to choose a path with heart is to learn how to follow intuitive feeling.
> **JEAN SHINODA BOLEN**

Inspired Action

At many times individuals, institutions, families and religions will try to tell us we are off track, and that we can only be saved by following *their* way. However, the great masters of wisdom and founders of religions have all discovered the truth of their Self for their self; and only sought to be guides pointing the way for others.

In *The Hierophant*, Ouspensky's 'great Master' says:

Seek the Path, do not seek attainment, Seek for the Path within yourself. Do not expect to hear the truth from others, nor to see it, or read it in books. Look for the truth in yourself, not without yourself. Aspire only after the impossible and inaccessible. Expect only that which shall not be. Do not hope for Me, do not look for Me, do not believe that I am outside yourself.

All the great masters lived from their true Self and were fluid in thought, feeling and action. Unfortunately, those who followed were often not at the same level of enlightenment and were therefore more rigid and rooted in their low self. Too often, even the most well-meaning of disciples clings on to the words of a master, but lacks full understanding of their meaning and uses them in inappropriate ways

When any church or guru suggests that they are the sole possessor of spiritual truth, if they try to discourage us from seeking the Kingdom within, and tell us to disregard our intuition, then they become the greatest deceiver of all and hold their flock in a small place.

In truth, no one can tell us for certain that they have 'the way'. Many will try. Many will turn to their religions and holy books saying: 'This is the word of God.' But of course it isn't. It is the word of man, written by the hand of man, and maybe that man or woman is flowing with the inspiration of God, but we don't know for sure. It is faith, not fact.

The beast in man is our low self devoid of our high Self. When our low self is without the guidance of our high Self, conscious and subconscious, thought and feeling, action and result are all divided, and the beast in man appears.

Active Faith

Learn to trust your Self and find your own way. It requires faith in your Self, self-awareness, self-acceptance and all the things that have gone in the pages before to truly follow your intuition. It can take a lifetime to apply consciously or a moment to live naturally. Practise on the little things first. Find the courage

> **Knowing is not enough; we must apply. Willing is not enough; we must do.**
> **GOETHE**

> **A little knowledge that acts, is worth infinitely more than much knowledge that is idle.**
> **KAHLIL GIBRAN**

> **I'm a great believer in luck and I find the harder I work, the more I have of it.**
> **THOMAS JEFFERSON**

> **Work joyfully and peacefully, knowing that right thoughts and right efforts will inevitably bring about right results.**
> **JAMES ALLEN**

to *act* on intuition and observe how the universe responds.

Many people come to depend on charms, chants, meditations and horoscopes to point the way. Like countless other touchstones, these are all simply ways of coming to our high Self and, through it, universal consciousness.

Find *your* way, follow it and show commitment by taking action. The universe applauds action.

For the last 15 years, since my awakening to personal development and the discovery of Spirit, I have lived a charmed and challenging life full of wondrous synchronicities. However, none of these things just happened; they were invariably attracted through action.

Self-transformation

Transformation of your self, from low to high, is best understood by rearranging the term into: self-trans-form-action, or *changing the form of your self through action*. The further I travelled along my path of personal development the more I saw of my low self and the more I realized I would need to consciously change many of my habits if I was to become my true Self.

In my search for answers and ideas I came across the teachings of the ancient alchemists who attempted to transform base metals into gold. The wisest of them learnt they would first need to transform their self. To achieve anything new in our lives will require transformation of our self in some way; transformation of a quality such as confusion into clarity, doubt into certainty, and procrastination into purposeful action. Our existence is a perpetual transformation of energies – mental, emotional, physical, financial, social and spiritual.

The Absolute gives birth to the world of multiplicity but all substance comes from one substance, transformed, multiplied and blended into many, and therefore all can be made into any.

Your high Self is the part of you that is connected to the One source of all knowledge, wisdom and creation. Let it be your guide and guru. Allow your high Self to guide your low self by sitting quietly and consciously connecting with your inner wisdom.

Find your own way. Simply observe your self – seek a state of non-attachment. Be a witness of everything and judge of nothing, not only of people and circumstance, but also with regard to your own thoughts, feelings and the physical body. Free your self of needing anything or anyone, including your self, to be any particular way. Just be.

By being still and connecting with our essence, we receive complete comfort from our high Self; we heal and integrate our selves, becoming whole.

> Who looks outside, dreams. Who looks inside, Awakens.
> **CARL JUNG**
>
> Happiness is a butterfly, which, when pursued, is always just beyond your grasp, but which, if you will sit down quietly, may alight upon you.
> **NATHANIEL HAWTHORNE**

– ◆ –

IN ESSENCE

The essence to remember and live from in this chapter is:

You must be the change
you wish to see in the world.

MAHATMA GANDHI

Creating Your Self Map

Still your self now, and engage in the final step of creating your Self Map.

Ask your self these freeing questions:

◆ What are the actions of my true Self?

◆ What actions or behaviours connect me with my high Self?

◆ What does my true Self *think* now, *feel* now, *do* now, *choose* now?

Step 7 –True-Self Picture

Well done. By engaging in the previous steps and asking your self the question 'Who am I?' you have raised your awareness and moved closer towards being your true Self. Even if you haven't filled in all of the statements from steps 1–6 you can still continue with the final step, Step 7, where real clarity and power is gained. It is now time to erase all of your low-self pencilled statements and draw over the spaces with pictures or symbols that represent your true-Self statements.

Symbols of Self

While it has become normal for most people to express their thoughts in words, it is actually natural for our subconscious and higher-conscious mind to think and process in pictures or symbols.

We think in pictures long before we learn to link them to words. Likewise, symbols are our most ancient form of communication and convey a depth of meaning that goes far beyond any written text.

To ensure that your intention to become your Self is deeply connected to your self and collective consciousness, it is now important that you turn your high-Self statements into corresponding drawings or pictures. By drawing over your low-self statements with high-Self pictures your low-self habits fade and your self is directed towards ever-greater development of your true Self.

Creating symbols, regardless of the quality of your drawing, is a powerful way of focusing the mind. Nobody else need know what your images mean. Self Mapping is a communication from your Self to your self. In Tibet this form of actualization is known as 'liberation through sight'. Only you need know what your symbol means. In my own experience I have discovered that the more simple the symbol, the more powerful it becomes.

> First keep the peace within yourself, then you can also bring peace to others.
> **THOMAS À KEMPIS**

To begin, place your two mandalas side by side. Rub out one of your low-self statements, and draw in a picture or symbol that represents your corresponding true-Self quality.

Take your time. Keep your pictures simple and use lots of colour. Only erase one low-self statement at a time, consciously letting go of it as you do so.

You can complete your Map all in one session or spread over a period of time. Once all of your written statements have been drawn as pictures, spontaneously choose a colour for the star in the very centre, a colour you believe represents the essence of your Self.

Pages 161–66 show some examples of the multi-coloured and joyous mandalas that have been created.

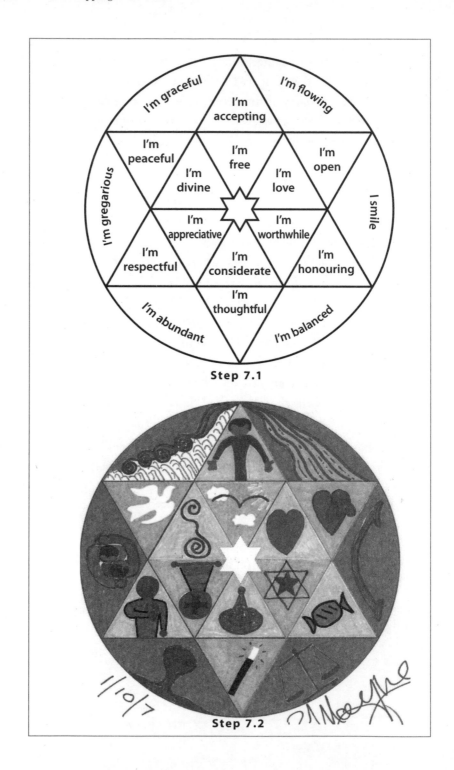

Step 7.1

Step 7.2

Chapter 8

Self-integration

All from One – and One from All

Everything comes from the One – one energy, one source, one point in time and space. Scientists call it 'the big bang' but in truth it was neither big nor a bang, just a tiny flicker of energy, smaller than the smallest particle, which has expanded to become our entire universe and everything in it. With great expansion has come great diversity; billions of different vibrations of light, sound and substance, creating countless varieties and forms of life, all interwoven and connected back to the One. We are each at our essence evolved from this One source, One energy, One consciousness – which spiritualists know as God.

The Diamond of Reality

The deepest truth of science or spirituality is that the essence of reality is pure vibrating energy and intelligence spiralling through endless cycles of evolution.

Imagine that the essence of reality is like the heart of a flawless diamond. Because of its purity it cannot be seen directly and instead must be observed as a reflection in the diamond's myriad facets. Through one facet reality shows itself as light, in another facet the same essence of reality can be observed as sound, in another it's transformed into gas, then liquid, continuing through the symphony of vibrational states that create substance in all its marvellous forms.

However, everything at its essence is made from the same core energy, the heart of the diamond. Only the rate of vibration shifts as the energy transforms itself into the different reflections of reality.

For example, if you add energy to ice by heating it, the energy of the heat causes the atoms to vibrate faster and change their state. The ice now transforms as it melts into water. Heat the water and the atoms vibrate even faster as they transform again into steam before evaporating into the air.

Every*thing* is made from no*thing*. All comes from the same core energy. In fact, in its purest form, the most concrete thing that can be said about matter is that it's more akin to a thought – a concentrated clump of energy and intelligence bound by intention.

Just as modern quantum physicists have discovered that at a subatomic level their own awareness can cause an effect in their experiments, so the sages of ancient times knew that a person's state of conscious is a cause that has an effect in their life. Reality can be affected by a single electron in the field of quantum physics or a single thought in the field of human consciousness. It is all part of the same universal ocean of energy and intelligence.

The Diamond of Self

There is an ancient truth, held sacred across all cultures and throughout history:

> As above, so below.

Tradition has it that Trismegistus Hermes uttered these words:

> True, without falsehood, certain, most certain.
> What is above is like what is below, and what is
>   below is like that which is above. To make
>   the miracle of the one thing.

And as all things were made from contemplation of one, so all things were born from one
adaptation.
Its father is the Sun, its mother is the Moon.
The wind carried it in its womb, the earth
breast fed it.
It is the father of all 'works of wonder' in the
world.
Its power is complete.

THE EMERALD TABLET

The One energy that everything comes from, including you and
me, is the pure pristine consciousness that can be seen in the
eyes of a newborn, the uninterrupted sparkle from the heart of
the diamond that is God.

Just as the essence of reality is like the heart of a flawless diamond, so we are each part of reality and therefore the diamond is
also at the heart of each of us, reflecting the essence
of our true Self.

The senses of sight, sound, touch, taste and smell
allow us to not only sample reality but also mix
what we receive with our own personal reality – our
beliefs, attitudes and behaviour. In this way we give
shine and brilliance to our own gem. And in turn,
who we are as a person becomes a facet in the greater diamond of reality. Our own personal light adds
to the brilliance of the whole.

> **The gem cannot be polished without friction, nor man perfected without trials.**
> **CHINESE PROVERB**

All people are born like natural diamonds.
By polishing our self, we bring out our
true brilliance.

Highs and Lows

By choosing to polish our low self we allow the guiding light in our heart to shine through from our high Self and add sparkle to our life. In this way we live from our true Self connected to the unity, the oneness, at the heart of the universe and we become of 'one mind'. Living from our true Self means living with an awareness of this oneness, feeling a sense of connection and harmony with our surroundings, people and the creative energies of life.

In Westminster Abbey, the tomb of the Unknown Soldier bears the inscription:

Be of one mind, and live in peace.

Poignant words for those that have lost their life in battle. For when we live from our low self, we are distracted from our true Self, become blind to the unity of life, and see only the differ-ences between our self and others. This fall into the pit of our ego disconnects us from the higher integrating, guiding, collect-ive consciousness that keeps us whole, and instead we increas-ingly become unsure of our self, erratic, mostly unconscious and generally of two minds.

As the high Self's motive is integration so the low self moves towards disintegration. When we fall really low in our self, we crash, and it seems like our world is coming apart. We fall to pieces, breaking mentally, emotionally and physically. The lower the self falls the more unrest and disintegration we experience. Our words and actions no longer match, our talk is not walked, the tongue is forked and the heart corked. Often we become two-faced, and eventually, when we sink really low, our personality splits. Instead of being One we become many: many minds, selves and faces, all separated, and therefore lacking in some way.

Being Whole

Self-integration is not only the natural prime purpose we are each born with, it is also the path of *wholeness* that brings the greatest riches into our lives. It is the path of true happiness, peace and abundance.

Whatever your current state of self-integration, or disintegration, wherever you are on your journey to becoming your true Self, you will make the most progress and achieve your highest rewards by drawing the aspects of your self together into greater wholeness.

Whether in a family, relationship or as an individual, becoming *whole* is the great prize of life. Look to your self first and foremost. By finding balance in your true Self, bringing your high Self and low self together, you create balance in your life and become a rock of stability helping others to find their balance also.

Balance in your self is only possible by having two halves. There must always be a yin to the yang. Without opposites, nothing would be different. The greater the *interactive* balance between the two the greater, more dynamic the whole.

Self-creation

Thoughts trigger feelings which in turn influence actions. Repeated thoughts form beliefs and shape our outlooks. Repeated feelings solidify into attitudes which direct our behaviours. And repeated behaviours create habit-patterns, all of which play their part in moulding your self and shaping your life.

In creating a Self Map we hold a core intention of being our true Self and thereby naturally live from the unifying energy of the universe. Continue to work with your Self Map and you will draw the aspects of your self together, and in so doing create 'synergy of self'.

Synergy means the *whole* is greater than the sum of its parts. The universe is synergistic. Balanced ecosystems are synergistic.

And, likewise, *you* are synergistic. The strands of a rope woven together are stronger than they are individually. The 'whole you' *integrated*, woven together, is greater than any aspect or strand of you.

A person who is on the path of self-integration leads from the light of their high-Self imagination and inspiration, while skilfully managing through low-self instinct and learnt behaviour. This natural balance enables them to be truly effective at envisioning their authentic desires and then taking the practical actions needed to create them in their self and life. They are spontaneous and free, while still pursuing a chosen path and purpose.

In this way, by combining the two halves, folding our low self into our high Self, we live with integrity and become whole, balanced and complete – our true Self, consciously connected to life and flowing in harmony with the current of creation.

Once again in the words of Jesus:

> When you make the two One,
> and you make the inner as the outer,
> and the outer as the inner,
> and the above as the below,
> so that you will make the male and female
> into a single One,
> in order that the male is not made male
> nor the female made female:
> when you make eyes into an eye,
> and a hand into a hand,
> and a foot into a foot,
> and even an image into an image,
> then shall you enter the Kingdom.

THE GOSPEL OF THOMAS

Make the Two One

Integrating our low self into our high Self helps to connect us with the oneness at the heart of life. Within the One everything has its opposite. Expansion is part of contraction. The pendulum swing manifests in all things. The measure of swing to the left is the measure of swing to the right.

All of creation, from a single atom through to an entire solar system, is an incredible interplay of energies, a *dance of polarities* summed up in the ancient symbol of the sacred marriage: the Hieros Gamos, which represents the divine play of opposites.

The two main entwined triangles symbolize the archetypes of masculine and feminine, the blade and the chalice. Sometimes they are referred to as fire and water. (The symbol corresponds to the yin and yang of Chinese philosophy.)

The sacred marriage

This sacred symbol is found in all manner of ancient shrines around the world particularly those of India where it represents the god Shiva and his consort Shakti. In addition it appears in the mystic writings of Judaism, known as the Seal of Solomon.

As above so below. As within so without. Drawing your high Self and low self together creates a second joining within your mind, that of your left-brain and right-brain thought processes, male and female qualities, management and leadership aspects. By combining the two, conscious and unconscious, spirit and ego, fear and love, we become *whole*, in mind, emotions, body and soul, and live from our integrated true Self.

All things are one.
HERACLITUS

The union of feminine and masculine energies within the individual is the basis of creation. Female intuition plus male action is creativity.
SHAKTI GAWAIN

Ritual

Throughout history and across all cultures, rituals of mind, emotion and action are the central system by which people have maintained traditions.

Rituals abound around the world, from the everyday greeting of shaking hands or nodding of heads, to the profound meaning-filled rituals of faiths and institutions, old and new. Since ancient times the essence of ritual within faith has been to anchor a little of heaven on earth. The whirling dervishes spin themselves into a trance in a bid to bridge heaven and earth; monks chant, shamans dance, and countless cultures use patterns, imagery and symbols to focus the mind and hold the intention.

> What I hear, I forget; What I see, I remember; But what I do, I understand.
> **CONFUCIUS**
>
> Merge with the world yet have the measure of all things.
> **MĀNDŪKYA UPANISHAD**

While the rituals may vary greatly, the essence stays basically the same: to draw your low self into your high Self so as to live from your true Self, every day and in all situations.

While retreating from the world, living in isolation, fasting and taking vows of chastity, silence and obedience may be part of some people's paths, ultimately we must learn to live in the real world, from the qualities of our true Self, anchored in our everyday life and situations, and thereby shine a light that helps illuminate a path for others around us.

Living the Self Mapping Ritual

The Self Map you have already created has helped hold your focus throughout the time you have been creating it. Drawing pictures or creating symbols that represent your intentions empowers and activates your right brain, which is the main gateway to your subconscious.

Whatever you drew on your Map, in the time you were drawing it you also held on the inside of your mind. Whether you were aware of it or not, drawing your Self Map was a way of focusing your mind on a picture of your true Self and thereby sending a command about who you choose to be.

The Self Map you have created works like a lens to focus your energy and hold your intention, in thought, feeling and action, to be your true Self, thereby anchoring a little of heaven on to earth.

Using your Self Map on a regular basis strengthens your self-command. Engage in the Self Mapping ritual by looking at your Map once or more each day, speaking aloud your statements and breathing between each one, and you connect your intentions at ever-greater levels and thereby pull your true Self even closer together.

Your Word Is Your Bond

The first step that will increase the power of your Self Map is to sign it. Your signature is your mark of commitment – it represents you saying you will *keep your word to your self* and follow through with your intentions. True commitment is not a one-off promise we give, but rather a choice we make in each and every moment. Choose to be your true Self in any situation or circumstance, simply by asking your self:

What would my true Self think now, feel now,
do now, choose now?

See It

Making a choice means staying aware that you have one, even in the heat of the moment. By visualizing your Self Map, either in your mind or by looking at it in a moment of quiet contemplation, you impress your intentions on to your consciousness and remind your self of what you hold to be most precious.

Place your Self Map somewhere visible to remind you to engage in the ritual of looking at it once or more each day. A bedroom wall is a good place as the best time to view your Map is first thing in the morning when your brain is still in alpha rhythm and the connection to your subconscious is over 100 times greater than it is at midday. (There are four basic brain frequencies or states. Alpha rhythm is generally held to be around 7.5 cycles per second. People naturally enter alpha when they first wake in the morning and just before sleep at night. It is widely agreed in the scientific community that this is the closest thing most people experience to deep meditation or hypnosis.) Likewise, the back of the bathroom door, side of the mirror or on the fridge are all great places for your Map.

I have scanned mine into my computer and use it as a screen-saver on my mobile phone. I've also printed off a couple and stuck one in the front of my journal, while the other is folded in my pocket. It is a constant reminder to me of what I know to be for my highest good.

> The secret of health for both mind and body is not to mourn for the past, worry about the future, or anticipate troubles ... but to live in the present moment wisely and earnestly.
>
> BUDDHA

Say It

As you visualize your Self Map, speak your intention *aloud* in the form of an affirmation such as, 'I am patient.' By seeing and stating your intentions as if they were already achieved – present tense, in the moment – you activate both your right and left brain and thereby powerfully command your sub-conscious self to make it so. While your conscious mind understands there is a past, present and future, your subconscious only lives in the moment of *now* and therefore responds best to commands phrased in present tense.

Breathe It

The English word 'spirit' comes from the Latin *spiritus*, meaning 'breath'. In India the Sanskrit word *prana*, the mystical life-force, also means breath. And the Mayan seal for 'spirit' is often depicted as 'breath on the tongue'.

Breathing in through the nose and out through the mouth, while visualizing and affirming your Map, helps to synchronize your left-brain low-self ego with your right-brain high-Self spirit, like two cogs turning together, conscious and subconscious, combining the two that you may see rightly and find your flow in life.

Try it now. Sit upright, lay your hands on your lap, palms up, with your thumb and first finger closed into a loop. Breathe in through your nose while looking at your first Self Map image, speak your affirmation, then look at your next picture, before breathing out through your mouth and speaking the corresponding statement. Repeat this exercise for all the actions or habits that appear around the outside of your mandala, breathing in on one, speaking it, then looking at the next and speaking it as you breathe out through your mouth. Take three breaths in total (in through the nose and out through the mouth) in order to cover the six habits stated in the outer circle of your mandala.

Now repeat the procedure for the next circle of qualities – your high-Self attitudes. This time curl your fingers on each hand round into two tubes, then again visualize your image. Breathe in, speak and repeat as before – three breaths covering the six attitudes.

Finally, change your finger position, laying your thumbs across your palms, closing your fingers around them, then visualize your top inner triangle covering your outlooks, and again breathe in, speak and repeat for three breaths to cover your six qualities.

Giving just a few moments each day to connect with our true Self in this way helps us anchor consciousness, stay more aware, live in the moment and choose what's best for our highest good and the highest good of all.

Henry Wadsworth Longfellow puts it poetically:

> The heights by great men reached and kept
> Were not attained by sudden flight,
> But they, while their companions slept,
> Were toiling upward in the night.

– ◆ –

IN ESSENCE

The essence to remember and live from in this chapter is:

Be the heart of the diamond.

Chapter 9

Self-renewal

Lord Let Me Be Made Anew

The above heading is a line from a popular nineties dance tune. It was a favourite of mine when I was a DJ and I played it often, although in truth I never really heard the words, let alone the *prayer* contained within them. Only years later, once I had opened my own eyes and was *made anew* in my self, seeing and living more from my true Self, did the meaning become clearer.

> To exist is to change, to change is to mature, to mature is to go on creating oneself endlessly.
> HENRI BERGSON

We are all, in fact, constantly being made anew. Growing hair, nails and skin are the most obvious signs of renewal. Every cell in our body replaces itself completely over the period of just a few years. There is not a part of you that you had more than seven years ago, and indeed, 60 per cent of you, the water you drink, will only be around six weeks old.

It's That Same Old Song...

The challenge is that we often unwittingly create the *new* in the form of the *old*. Our low-self ego fears change and therefore holds on to the same old song, notions, beliefs, attitudes and habits, desperately wanting things to continue unaltered; it fears that any transformation of low self to high Self would mean its death. Because the mental directs the emotional and influences the physical, it means we often end up with more of the same, both in our self and our life, whether we consciously want it or not.

As Sara Paddison points out in *The Hidden Power of the Heart*:

> You only hurt yourself when you're not expanding and growing. Many people can't stand the thought of aging, but it's the crystallized thought patterns and inflexible mind-sets that age people before their time. You can break through and challenge your crystallized patterns and mind-sets. That's what evolution and the expansion of love are really about.

Only by being made anew in our Self, changing our low-self outlooks, attitudes and actions for those of our true Self, do we really see the new. And not just new in terms of what we create or attract in our self and life, but also in what we reveal, the beauty, joy and happiness that was in fact always there within and around us.

At a relatively early stage of my personal development journey I encountered some experiences so profound that overnight my outlook, attitudes and actions completely shifted. The change was so dramatic that many of my friends and family were actually worried about me, whereas in my self I felt blessed. Before that point I had never really been aware of the natural beauty of a cloud, or a flower, let alone perceived the magnificence that lies at the heart of people. It was like a whole other reality had opened up, one that had always been there in the people, places and principles of life, but that I, my ego and my low self, had been completely oblivious to.

Try Something New Today

In reality, although our low-self resists it, change is not only good for us but vital for our true well-being. Without change within our body we would die. And without change in the universe it would freeze. Total sameness equals stagnation and death.

Likewise in our mind and emotions we need to try on new ways of being as we move through the ever-changing scenery of our low self on our journey to being our true Self. My baby daughter Ayesha still greets change with her high-Self childlike curiosity and is completely enthralled by the absolute wonder of it all. Meanwhile, her five-year-old sister Shanti, who is now busy forming an ego with all its set beliefs, attitudes and habits, already wants a lot of things to stay the same. Even at her tender age, unless she is inspired by a picture of receiving some future pleasure or comfort, she doesn't try anything new at all, especially where food is concerned.

Regardless of age, the key for true well-being, in mind, heart, body and life, is not only to greet change with a positive expectation, holding an image, picture or intention of where we want to go, what we want to do and who we choose to become, but much more than that, to hold a picture of our self being our Self.

It is only by inspiring our low self to merge with our high Self that we stay connected to the unchanging core at the heart of our being, our true Self, which becomes a rock of stability while everything around us may change rapidly. This is the prime goal of life that each of us is born with – and it is the path of enlightenment.

Where the Wind Blows

Within my various workshops, particularly those on one of my other systems, Goal Mapping, I often meet people who tell me they don't really like setting goals. They want to 'stay free and easy, see what shows up in life, and be spontaneous'. It is an admirable quality and one which I endeavour to accomplish myself, however, it is also important to realize that 'being free and easy' is in fact a goal in its own right.

Indeed, pretty much everything we do and every way that we can be, including spontaneous, is a goal in some form or other. Whether conscious or unconscious, we create mental pictures of who we choose to be which in turn form commands for our subconscious and universal consciousness to make it so. Any way that we are, anything that we do, or result we create, doesn't just happen by accident – it is an *effect* which is *caused* by the thought-picture blueprints we carry in our head. Without goals, intentions or purpose we would simply cease to be.

All of life has a goal – it's the primeval drive of evolution, the urge to move forwards, grow and become more. As humans we are unique in that we are each blessed with the divine gift of free will and can therefore choose our own way, set our own direction, pursue our desired intentions. And of all the noblest of goals and worthy aims we can choose to hold, the greatest are intentions about the development of our self; *who we choose to become*. For it is through our *self* that we touch every other area, person and aspect of our life.

> If you do not conquer self, you will be conquered by self.
> **NAPOLEON HILL**

Who Are You, and Who Do You Choose to Be?

As you continue to work with your Self Map you will become more and more conscious of your habits. By observing without judgement or justification the fruits of your own or another's actions you gain an insight into the dominant outlooks and attitudes that lie under the surface.

Being aware of your habits is the first step in choosing those that serve you and dropping those that don't. If you are not aware of them, then instead of you having your habits, your habits really have you, and dictate your limitations.

Many times we will intend to do our best and seek to live by spiritual values, perhaps becoming involved in worthy and wonderful work, but like a chain we are only as strong as our weakest link. When tough times come, things go wrong and the pressure is on, we more easily slip back into the self-destructive habit-patterns of the low self in our struggle to find comfort.

One of the strongest low-self patterns for me has been losing my temper and shouting. Like all habits it will have a trigger point followed by a thought that then triggers the next link in the chain creating a feeling and eventually influencing an action. If the action is negative, which it usually is, it is quickly followed by some form of negative, reactive self-talk: 'You're such a loser. Why do you always do that?' Regardless of the particular wording used, the sentiment is always self-defacing and critical. Such thoughts will make anyone feel bad about himself; and not caring about our self, we spiral down even further into our low self to repeat the action again.

> Once the principle of movement has been supplied, one thing follows on after another without interruption.
> **ARISTOTLE**

Insight

Without question, the most rewarding practice or ritual I've engaged in over the years is to sit quietly with my journal for a few moments. I visualize, breathe and speak my Self Map, which is pasted inside the front cover of my journal, then put pen to paper allowing whatever thoughts that surface to flow out. Using this ritual I have reached states where I am better able to ask my high Self questions about my low self and my situation, and receive inner insight and guidance about the best path to take.

It requires courage to follow our own guidance as our low self always wants reassurance from outside. By finding the courage to take the step, even if it's only to follow through on the little things, the casual hunches and intuitions we receive, we gain faith in our Self and gradually build self-reliance.

> Dare to ask, be willing to listen, and prepare to act. For the vision of our future emerges as the world of spirit awakens.
> **RUSSELL DESMARAIS**

Out of Your Mind and into Your Heart

Learn to listen to your heart. Place your consciousness there and be aware of the subtle changes that take place as you ask and answer your own questions. While our head will tell us many things, often chasing round in circles with justifications and excuses, our heart will always speak truthfully.

By investing just a few moments in our low self each day, we gradually become more conscious and accelerate our journey to becoming our true Self. The more you immerse your self in your Self Map, first thing in the morning while your mind is still open, the more empowered you will be in your Self and enriched in your life.

The great Sufi mystic Rumi shares his wisdom:

> To go out of our minds at least once a day is tremendously important. By going out of your mind you come to your senses! When you come out of the conditioned, limited and unaware mind the centre of gravity naturally shifts to the heart.
> **ALAN WATTS**

The breeze at dawn has secrets to tell you. Don't go back to sleep. You must ask for what you really want. Don't go back to sleep. People are going back and forth across the door seal where the two worlds touch. The door is round and open. Don't go back to sleep. The door is round and open. Don't go back to sleep.

Share It

I have now been living and sharing this material for many years and it has been life-changing for me. Writing this book has helped me move to another level of awareness and integration of my self.

This principle holds true for anyone and for anything we may want to learn: by teaching it to others we come to understand it more fully ourselves. Often we will think we know something well, and it is only when we come to share it with another that we realize that we haven't quite mastered it; and it makes us stretch for a deeper level of understanding.

Download the free Self Mapping templates from the website selfmapping.co.uk and share the system with someone you care about. You don't need to explain the whole philosophy unless you want to; simply guide them through the creation of their own Self Map, and both of you will be benefitted in the process.

Repeat It

You may discover that you want to create another Self Map, as in the process of producing it you have activated a deeper consciousness and since come up with greater insights into your self and Self. If so please follow through with your intuition and create a second Self Map, or simply update your first. This will help take your intention and insight to a still deeper place.

Regardless of whether you have new insights now, or are content with your Map, I strongly recommend that you print out two additional Self Mapping templates, one for your high Self and the other for your low self, and place them somewhere that allows you to add new insights as and when you receive them.

> Thousands of candles can be lighted from a single candle, and the life of the candle will not be shortened. Happiness never decreases by being shared.
>
> **BUDDHA**

In this way you gradually build up and maintain an overall insight of who you are and who you choose to be. Then, when the time feels right, you can quickly create a new Self Map as you will already have the statements or qualities recorded.

Another way to use Self Mapping is to create a focused Map for a specific area of your life. For example, a Self Map is a great companion while progressing through a diet, cleansing or fitness programme. Likewise, Self Maps can be created for being your best with regard to a new venture, project or plan. Simply focus your Map on the qualities that are most supportive of you achieving your goal, by asking your Self: 'Who do I need to be to achieve this?' Then capture your insights as before in both words and pictures.

Whatever you choose as the focus for your particular Map, some of the fundamental qualities which are likely to appear are: courageous, persistent, committed, motivated, active, etc. You may even find that many of the qualities you identify are already on your main Map and that your focused map is only slightly different. However, that slight difference can make a huge difference when it comes to successfully achieving your goal.

In addition, and for even greater clarity and power, you can combine your Self Map with another of my success systems, Goal Mapping, which is designed to help you stay mindful of your purpose, goals and specific actions. Together, Self Mapping and Goal Mapping cover the fundamental success principle of Be, Do, Have and help you maintain a positive focus on your Self and throughout all the areas and aspects of your life.

Trust It

Consider feedback and guidance from everyone, but do not follow those who describe the journey but are not on the trip themselves. They are only reading the maps of another. If you want a guide, find someone who knows the scenery intimately. Above all else, learn to trust in your self, your own insight and hunches. We must each find our own way – what is best for us.

> We must learn to reawaken and keep ourselves awake, not by mechanical aids, but by an infinite expectation of the dawn.
>
> **HENRY DAVID THOREAU**

> I know that the answer to what we need to do next is in our own hearts. All we have to do is listen, then … trust what we hear.
>
> **MELODY BEATTIE**

All Is God

The true goal of life, the prime reason for being, is to give your low self to your high Self, the god within you, and become your true Self.

Follow the diamond at the heart of your Self and, like a personal guiding star, it will guide you back home, gradually expanding your Self until its natural radiance eclipses the flicker of your self to become your true Self.

Be still now, my friend, and know you are God. I am God. All is God, and *God is All*.

May peace, happiness, abundance and complete comfort be within you.

And the day came when the risk it took to remain tight inside the bud was more painful than the risk it took to blossom.

ANAIS NIN

Appendices

Self Mapping Template

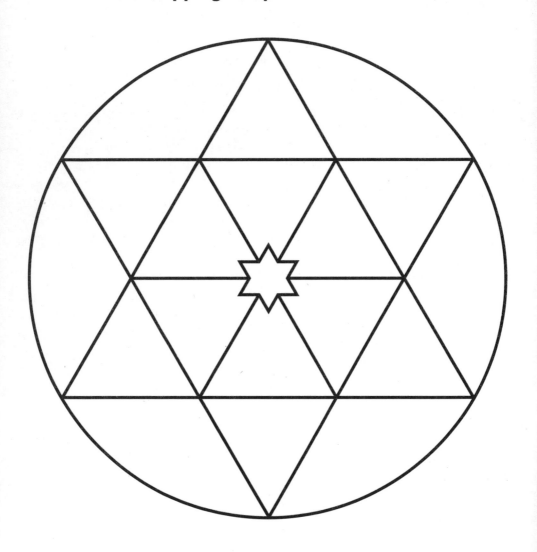

Recommended Reading

Related Titles

Goal Mapping – Brian Mayne (Watkins, 2006)

Goal Mapping is a practical workbook that trains you in a highly original system for achievement and shows you how to apply it to any objective or goal. Whatever your dream, *Goal Mapping* can help you achieve it.

Sam the Magic Genie – Brian Mayne (Vermilion, 2003)

The enchanting story centres on a young boy who is visited one night by a magical genie called Sam who represents his subconscious. Together they go on an adventure exploring the world of *thoughts* and how they turn into *feelings* and *things*.

The Seven Magic Keys for Success – Brian Mayne (Brian Mayne Limited 2018)

This life-skills programme is based on *Sam the Magic Genie* combined with *Goal Mapping* and is ideal for children of all ages. Designed to be used by parents or teachers, the pack includes adult and student workbook, plus one copy of *Sam the Magic Genie*.

Life Mapping – Brian and Sangeeta Mayne (Vermilion, 2002)

Life Mapping is the sister technique to Goal Mapping and follows the same basic principles of left-brain words and right-brain pictures, only instead of being focused on the achievement of 'things', *Life Mapping* is dedicated to helping you develop empowering 'qualities of character'. Together the two techniques cover the fundamental success principle of *Be-Do-Have*: *Be* your best in your self, which will naturally lead you to *Do* your best work, and *Have* your best results.

Further Reading

Attwood, Janet Bray and Attwood, Chris, *The Passion Test*, Simon & Schuster, 2007.

Buzan, Tony, *The Mind Map Book: Radiant Thinking – Major Evolution in Human Thought*, BBC, 2003.

Chopra, Deepak, *The Seven Spiritual Laws of Success: A Practical Guide to the Fulfillment of Your Dreams*, Bantam, 1996.

Coelho, Paulo, *The Alchemist*, HarperCollins, 1991.

Dyer, Wayne W, *You'll See It When You Believe It*, Arrow, 2005.

Frankl, Victor E, *Man's Search for Meaning*, Beacon, 2000.

Gangaji, *The Diamond in Your Pocket*, Cygnus, 2005.

Hoff, Benjamin, *The Tao of Pooh*, Methuen, 1984.

Khanna, Madhu, *Yantra: The Tantric Symbol of Cosmic Unity*, Thames & Hudson, 1981.

MacCuish, Savitri, Patel, Mansukh and Jones, John, *Walking with the Bhagavad Gita*, Life Foundation Publications, 1998.

Maltz, Maxwell, *Psycho-cybernetics*, Simon & Schuster, 1960.

McGregor Ross, Hugh, *The Gospel of Thomas*, Watkins, 2002.

McTaggart, Lynne, *The Intention Experiment: Use Your Thoughts to Change the World*, HarperElement, 2007.

Robbins, Anthony, *Awaken the Giant Within*, Pocketbooks, 2001.

Shearer, Alistair and Russell, Peter, *The Upanishads*, Bell Tower, 2003.

Tolle, Eckhart, *A New Earth: Awakening to Your Life's Purpose*, Penguin, 2006.

Walsch, Neale Donald, *Conversations with God: An Uncommon Dialogue*, Hodder Mobius, 1997.

Zukav, Gary, *The Dancing Wu Li Masters: Overview of the New Physics*, Rider, 1979.

Courses and Contact Information

Goal Mapping Online

Watch informative video on the principles of success, receive
daily inspiring quotes, engage in interactive exercises and
create powerful Goal Maps in words and pictures with this
free, fast and effective program. www.goalmapping.com/
register

*Goal Mapping, Life Mapping and Self Mapping Workshops,
Keynote Presentations, and Trainer Accreditation
Programmes* are run on a regular basis for businesses,
schools and the general public. If you are interested in
attending a presentation or becoming a Goal Mapping prac-
titioner please contact Brian Mayne Limited, details below.

Brian Mayne Limited
www.goalmapping.com
info@goalmapping.com

Index

WATKINS
Sharing Wisdom Since 1893

The story of Watkins began in 1893, when scholar of esotericism John Watkins founded our bookshop, inspired by the lament of his friend and teacher Madame Blavatsky that there was nowhere in London to buy books on mysticism, occultism or metaphysics. That moment marked the birth of Watkins, soon to become the publisher of many of the leading lights of spiritual literature, including Carl Jung, Rudolf Steiner, Alice Bailey and Chögyam Trungpa.

Today, the passion at Watkins Publishing for vigorous questioning is still resolute. Our stimulating and groundbreaking list ranges from ancient traditions and complementary medicine to the latest ideas about personal development, holistic wellbeing and consciousness exploration. We remain at the cutting edge, committed to publishing books that change lives.

DISCOVER MORE AT:
www.watkinspublishing.com

Read our blog   Watch and listen to   Sign up to
our authors in action   our mailing list

We celebrate conscious, passionate, wise and happy living.
Be part of that community by visiting

 /watkinspublishing    @watkinswisdom
 /watkinsbooks    @watkinswisdom